CHINAGLIA!

Giorgio
Chinaglia

with
BASIL KANE

Simon and Schuster
New York

Library of Congress Cataloging in Publication Data

Chinaglia, Giorgio, 1947–
  Chinaglia!

   Includes index.
   1. Chinaglia, Giorgiò, 1947–
2. Soccer players—Italy—Biography. I. Kane,
Basil G., joint author.
GV942.7.C53A32   796.334′092′4 [B]   80–11653

ISBN 0–671–25049–3

ACKNOWLEDGMENTS

Of all the people who helped me write this book I must single out my wife, Connie, as the one to whom I am most indebted. Not only did she help me remember places, dates, people and anecdotes but she was also very understanding and supportive during the many months of writing this book. My thanks also go to my children, Cynthia, George Jr., and Stephanie, for their patience while their father's study door was closed.

I am also extremely grateful to my many friends both here and in Italy who have been an invaluable help to me in writing this book; to Basil Kane, for helping me express best what I wanted to say; to Jonathan Segal, my editor at Simon and Schuster, for his wise counsel and unending enthusiasm; and to my manager and friend, Peppe Pinton, for always being there when I needed help.

to Tommaso Maestrelli

INTRODUCTION

PEOPLE BORN AS I WAS in Carrara, a small town in the Tuscany region of Italy, have had the reputation for centuries of saying exactly what's on their minds. A quick glance at all the trouble I've found myself in during my nineteen-year soccer career would make it obvious that I've inherited the Carrara characteristics of honesty and bluntness.

My Carrara candor has gotten me into hot water many times over the years. When I was 16 I nearly found myself out of professional soccer forever following a verbal confrontation with Trevor Morris, the manager at Swansea Town in the English second division; at 19 I was in trouble again when I let the management at Massese in the Italian third division know just what I thought about their training methods; by the age of 21 I had already caused a ruckus in the clubhouse of Internapoli, another Italian third-division club; and at Lazio, in the Italian first division, I was repeatedly in the doghouse with both the management and the Italian press during my seven-year stay there.

In both Italy and the United States much has been writ-

ten about my "inferference" with both Lazio's and the
Cosmos' coaching and managerial responsibilities. My
"meddling" with the Lazio front office saw me accused of
getting rid of a coach and picking the weekly lineups,
while on this side of the ocean the news media claim I
had something to do with the resignations of Ken Furphy,
Gordon Bradley, and Clive Toye and in the hiring of
Eddie Firmani. In recent months some imaginative writers have been spreading tales that I am heading a drive to
have Phil Woosnam replaced as the NASL commissioner.

Because of these and other media inaccuracies most of
the soccer world thinks of Giorgio Chinaglia as the most
arrogant, powerful, and Draconian individual ever to kick
a soccer ball for a living.

As a misunderstood player throughout my soccer career,
I think it's about time I sat down and wrote something in
my defense. Perhaps in the next few hundred pages I may
be able to counter my critics' charges and prove that my
undeserved reputation is based upon a lifetime of others'
refusing to accept my outspoken honesty and candor.

Soccer has been more than good to me: I've met many
wonderful people, seen a good deal of the world, and enjoyed most of the best things of life. So as my playing days
draw to an end I can think of no better way to repay some
of my debts to the simple but splendid game than by opening up my heart and mind to soccer fans both here and
abroad.

Giorgio Chinaglia
Englewood, New Jersey
December 1979

CHAPTER 1

I LIKE TO THINK I have a keen sense of humor and a knack for seeing the funny side of the most difficult of situations but on May 20, 1979, as I waited nervously in the tunnel of Giants Stadium for my name to be announced, I was probably the gloomiest person in New Jersey. Ironically, it was Giorgio's Day, a memorable milestone in my life and a day which I had awaited eagerly since the Cosmos first planned it a few months earlier. It should have been one of the happiest days in my soccer career but the longer I stood in the tunnel, nearly oblivious to the greetings and congratulations of friends and celebrities around me, the more tense I became. What I had been dreading all week was about to happen.

Jim Karvellas, who handles the Cosmos' TV play-by-play so ably, was ending his introductory remarks and any moment he would give me my cue to run onto the field up to the raised dais where Ahmet Ertegun, the Cosmos president, and other dignitaries were waiting for me. Karvellas would say "Please welcome Giorgio Chinaglia"—and then the boos would echo around the magnificent 76,000-seat stadium.

I have played professional soccer since I was 15, been on four championship teams, played in fourteen internationals, and scored over 450 goals in top-class soccer, yet all I could think about on this festive day was how loud would the booing be.

Actually, booing or jeering had never bothered me much until I came to the Cosmos. Like all professional athletes, I had learned to accept the right of paying audiences to express their feelings, regardless of how irresponsible or ill founded they might be. But the situation at the Cosmos' home games was unlike anything I had seen in soccer before. It defied the old soccer tradition that home fans do not get on their own players, particularly if they are successful.

"Giorgio Chinaglia!"

My legs felt like two leaden stilts as I trotted out of the tunnel. A loud booming cheer accompanied me on my way to the dais on the halfway line. I looked neither to my right nor to my left for fear that a glance at the stands would be the cue for the anti-Chinaglia group to express themselves with their usual rudeness. And then, just as I neared the smiling faces of my wife, Connie, Ahmet Ertegun, and the others on the dias I heard the hecklers for the first time. Fortunately, the faint chorus of boos was barely audible amid the cheers and applause.

But by the time I grasped Ahmet's outstretched hand, the boos had grown in volume and were nearly rivaling the cheers. It so unsettled me I was hardly aware of the flattering speeches or the beautiful gifts being handed to me.

At first I felt hurt and kind of stupid standing there being honored by my club while some of its fans made it clear they didn't like it very much. But the longer I stood on the dais, the more my mood changed from self-pity to anger. These so-called Cosmos fans, through their ignorance and stupidity, sickened me but at the same time made me determined to continue scoring more goals than any-one else in the NASL.

I suppose I was naive at the beginning of the season to have expected the booing to stop after my successful 1978 season. After breaking the 30-goal NASL goalscoring record held jointly by John Kowalik and Pepe Fernandez, set in 1968, I assumed the booing was a thing of the past. But the booing in 1979 was if anything louder than in 1978 or 1977. It was as if my goalscoring spree in 1978 (60 goals in 59 games—with 34 goals in the regular season, five in the playoffs, and 21 in exhibition games) had made the anti-Chinaglia group angrier than ever. No longer simply a matter of retaliating for some of my outspoken statements to the press, the booing seemed to suggest that there was a permanent feud between me and a few thousand fans.

Although there's no way I can prove it, I suspect the anti-Chinaglia forces mainly comprise some of those foreign-born fans who have never forgiven the NASL for entering into their once private world of soccer, where tensions from ancient nationalistic feuds and past foreign wars could be released on Sunday afternoons.

It was these ethnics who became enraged when I suggested that the 35-year-old Pelé was no longer functioning on all eight cylinders when I first played with him in 1976. They also thought I had broken one of the ten commandments in 1977 when I said in all honesty that the Cosmos did not need a sweeper like Franz Beckenbauer but an attacking midfielder. And when David Hirshey, that fine soccer writer, quoted me in *Sport* early in 1979 to the effect that those ethnics were a bunch of idiots it was obvious why the booing had increased. I always speak the truth and quite often the truth hurts.

At the conclusion of the pregame ceremonies I made a short speech in which I thanked the Cosmos, the fans, and those assembled on the dais for their kindness and for the great honor bestowed on me. While I was speaking, I noticed that the NASL commissioner, Phil Woosnam, was not among the dignitaries. The commissioner rarely misses an opportunity to be seen on such occasions so I figured he was still upset about my remarks quoted in *Sport*—not only those about the ethnics but also my saying that the commissioner's office was ineffective. For weeks he had been insisting that I should make an apology to him, to the league, and to all the foreign-born American soccer fans. I had been misquoted concerning the commissioner's office, and I had no intention of apologizing for what I believed to be the truth about the ethnics. I have never done so before, not even during the 1974 World Cup in West Germany, when in similar circumstances I refused to buckle under to administration threats even though my Italian soccer career hung in the balance.

The serious predicament I found myself in during the '74 World Cup stemmed from a signal I made to the cheering fans as I left the field in Munich after being substituted for. I had only wanted the fans to stop cheering since I knew I hadn't played well, but my coach and the national team officials all claimed I had made a defiant and obscene gesture.

I was very unhappy with both my performance and that of my teammates on that evening in Munich's Olympic Stadium. Here we were, one of the top national teams in the world, unbeaten for two years and filled with such world-class talent as Dino Zoff, Giacinto Facchetti, Tarcisio Burgnich, Gianni Rivera, Sandro Mazzola, and Luigi Riva, and yet semiprofessionals from one of the smallest soccer-playing countries in the world, Haiti, were making us look bad. Most of the 65,000 fans in the stadium were Italians and they didn't at all mind showing their disapproval of our lackluster showing.

In front of a TV audience estimated to be 350 million, I missed two easy chances in the first ten minutes. Nevertheless, I was not too concerned since it was clear that the Haitians were no match for us. But as the game progressed, the better the Haitians played and the shakier we became. We still hadn't scored by halftime, and with the score still 0–0 there were more than a few worried faces among my teammates as we walked back to the locker room.

One minute after the interval a thunderbolt struck in the form of Emmanuel Sanon, the speedy Haitian left winger. Collecting a ball near the penalty area, he swept through out defense like a hot knife through butter to score a spectacular goal. Mighty Italy, World Cup champion in 1934 and '38 and runner-up in 1970, was losing, 1–0, to tiny Haiti. Our Italian fans were stunned into silence. Was this going to be a repeat of the remarkable defeat of Italy by the unknown North Koreans in the 1966 World Cup? Adding to the drama of the moment was the fact that this surprise goal was the first scored against Italy since 1972. It was also the first time in 13 games that our goalie, Dino Zoff, had been forced to reach into the back of the net.

Haiti's goal roused us from our lethargy; four minutes later Gianni Rivera equalized and Romeo Benetti put us ahead in the 66th minute. But our team still lacked unison and we knew that to win against Haiti was not enough; we had to score six or more goals since we expected the two other powerful teams in our group, Argentina and Poland, would do so when they faced Haiti.

It was about this time that I noticed striker Pietro Anastasi warming up along the touchline. Since both Luigi Riva and I were struggling to find our true form, I started to wonder which one of us coach Ferruccio Valcareggi would take out. With one eye on Anastasi and one on the game, I lost my concentration and took an impossible shot from near the goal line with Riva in a perfect position to score.

Valcarregi took me out right after this. Anastasi ran on and I walked off to a surprising round of applause. It was then that I made the fateful sign. I raised my forefingers in an attempt to stop undeserved cheering from the loyal Italian fans. I knew I had played poorly and no one is harder on Chinaglia than I am when I have performed below my expectations.

I was very upset with myself, and when I reached the dressing room and saw some water bottles neatly lined up on the trainer's table I threw each one against the wall in disgust.

As far as I was concerned that was the end of my burst of anger. Consider then the shock I felt when Valcareggi and the Italian soccer federation officials came into the dressing room after the game and accused me of disgracing the team, the Italian federation, and even the Italian flag by gesturing in such an obscene way at the fans when leaving the field. In addition, they claimed I had been throwing water bottles at innocent people.

Suddenly, I found myself ostracized. Only my two fellow Lazio teammates on the squad, Pino Wilson and Luciano Re Cecconi, would talk to me. On the train back to Stuttgart the next day things got worse. Every ten minutes or so the federation officials held meetings to discuss my punishment. Pino Wilson overheard one of their discussions in which it was suggested I be sent home to Italy at once.

At the hotel that night I was informed that there would be a press conference the next morning, and I was ordered to be ready to apologize to the Italian people for my unforgivable behavior. In no uncertain terms I told Valcareggi and Italo Allodi, the manager of the team, that I could think of nothing to apologize for other than my poor performance in the game.

At two o'clock the next morning the angry federation officials flew in from Rome my Lazio coach and dear friend Tommaso Maestrelli to see what he could do. Tommaso was concerned that if I spoke too critically at the press conference I would be barred from the 1974–75 season. He pointed out that as defending champion each game Lazio played would be like a championship playoff, and that to lose me for the season would be a disaster for him and my Lazio teammates. "You don't have to lie to please them, Giorgio, but for God's sake be diplomatic."

Having always trusted Tommaso's counsel I agreed to control my emotions and the next day I told a packed room of TV, radio, and newspaper reporters that despite what the federation might say about the incident, as far as I was concerned I had done nothing to bring the game of soccer into disrespect and that I could think of no reason for all the fuss.

Speaking the truth has always been the best policy for me. I heard nothing more about being sent home or being suspended. The only noticeable lasting effect of the 1974 World Cup tempest in a teapot was that I encountered more than the usual amount of hostility from the northern players on the team, but relations between the teams of Milan and Turin and those from Rome have never been very harmonious anyway.

In the spring of 1979 I had already decided that I would treat Commissioner Woosnam's charges against me in the same manner I did the federation's accusations in the '74 World Cup. I would tell the truth and damn the consequences. Some of my friends, repeating their advice in 1974, argued that it would be better to acquiesce and do whatever was necessary to stay in the good graces of the ruling soccer body. I can't accept that proposition. As long as I can remember, I've been compulsive when it comes to saying exactly what I feel. It's just not in my makeup to hedge or to be tactful. It is simply more natural for me to be forthright. My mother says I was the same way even when I was five and dismaying the nuns at school in Carrara.

Carrara, a quaint town of 80,000, fifty miles northeast of Florence and a few miles off the Tyrrhenian coast, is the center of the world's most famous marble works. People born there are supposed to be as hard as its beautiful white marble. Michelangelo spent many years of his life in Carrara supervising the workers in the quarries and this is, of course, a source of great pride to the townspeople.

I was born there on January 24, 1947, many miles from the nearest hospital and many light-years away from ambulances, Blue Cross, Blue Shield, and baby formulas. My mother gave birth to me on an old bed supplied by my dear grandmother, while a local midwife, for a fee of $2, performed all the specialized skills needed for such an auspicious occasion. A few hours later a wet nurse was called in to feed me since my mother was unable to provide me with sufficient milk. And no wonder. Neither she nor the rest of us ever got enough to eat. The depression in Italy following World War II had left its heavy mark on Carrara. Of the twenty-six people living in my grandmother's house only one, an uncle of mine, had a job. If my grandmother had not owned the house, our family would have been forced to split up long before my father reluctantly decided to leave his beloved Italy and apply for a job in the British iron and steel industry.

Whenever I feel depressed and upset, all I have to do to remind myself of my present good fortune is think back to those meager meals we ate in Carrara. Around a big marble table (marble was cheap and plentiful then) all my relatives would sit trying to decide which choice to make from the two my grandmother offered: either a piece of bread or an egg along with milk with a little drop of coffee in it. Grandma's chickens were our lifeline—without them who knows how we would have survived. (Unfortunately, one of her chickens was diseased and my sister Rita developed yellow jaundice.) Occasionally we had a pasta dish but only when my uncle, who was a bus driver, could afford it out of his scanty salary.

We ate a little better when my father began to send money orders to my mother from Wales. But most of his surplus money was saved to pay for her fare to join him, which she did in 1953.

My sister and I stayed in Carrara with my grandmother until my parents could afford to send us our fares. It took three more years before they had saved enough to do that.

While I waited I played soccer. Big for my age, I was able to hold my own against my nine- and ten-year-old friends. From the very beginning I wanted to score goals.

Once I scored a goal while playing near a marble factory. My 10-year-old friend Valsega, upset that I had scored against him, insisted that I go get the ball which had fallen into a stream used to cool off the marble. Normally, in the summer, the water is at a low level, but that year must have been unusual for when I jumped in I went under. It was typical Hollywood drama, for not only couldn't I swim but the current began to force me toward the huge mechanical saws the factory used to cut the marble. Fortunately, Valsega grabbed me by the hair and pulled me out in time.

When my parents heard of this incident they decided it was time for Rita and me to join them in Wales, a place that Rita and I considered a land of plenty, for my grandmother had told us our parents were consuming enormous quantities of fish and fried potatoes there. Yes, we agreed it must be a virtual paradise, for why else would our parents leave the beautiful Apuan Alps around Carrara and the blue waters of the Mediterranean?

It took us two days to go from Carrara to Genoa to
Milan to Calais to Folkestone to London, and finally to
Cardiff. When we arrived there in the middle of the night
there were no buses or cabs available to drive us to our
new home. Finally, after much searching, my father found
a postoffice employee who, for a handful of English cur-
rency, allowed us to travel in the back of his van amid
the bags of letters and parcels.

I fell asleep before we arrived at 111 Richmond Road.
It would be a mild understatement to say I was terribly
disappointed upon awakening to discover I was sleeping
on a canvas campbed, next to another campbed which in
turn was parked next to a double bed. I reassured myself
that the all-too-familiar sleeping arrangement was just
temporary, but it was soon made clear to me that I had
exchanged a crowded house for a crowded one-room
apartment.

Our landlady was a middle-aged Italian entrepreneur by
the name of Mrs. Robatto. She rented out our one-room
flat at the then exorbitant rate of five pounds a week ($14)
which in Wales in the early fifties was the average weekly
salary for unskilled workers. As a matter of fact, it was
exactly the sum my mother earned working 42 hours a
week in a restaurant kitchen. Because both my parents
worked, Mrs. Robatto was also paid extra to watch my
sister and me during working hours. Her idea of lunch
was a bowl of wheatabix or shredded wheat. She filled her
son's bowl to the brim with milk and sugar but my sister
and I were forced to eat the dry, throat-gagging cereal
straight. Complaining wouldn't have done any good and
we didn't want to bother Mother, for we both realized how
tired she was when she came home at night. Anyway, we
were so happy to see her come in the door that our day's
problems were soon forgotten.

Mrs. Robatto's house was in the Roth Park area of
Cardiff, one of the best neighborhoods in the city. Vic-

torian architecture dominated the tree-lined streets. Most of the structures were four-story row houses. When they were built in the nineteenth century they were intended for one family and three or four servants, the typical "Upstairs, Downstairs" setup. The housing shortage caused by the bombing of World War II had put an end to that arrangement, and now each floor of these stately homes was a one- or two-family apartment. Although Mrs. Raubatto had gone one better with her one-room apartment, my parents were still grateful to be her tenants since small children were not welcome in the tight apartment market.

We lived at Richmond Road until 1960, by which time my parents had saved enough for us to move to a five-room apartment on Talbot Street. Money was still scarce in the Chinaglia household since my father had left the iron works to become an apprentice cook at the Royal Hotel, probably the finest hotel in Wales at that time. In today's parlance Dad was a workaholic. Fourteen hours a day was the norm for him. I can't remember him ever working less than fourteen hours a day, either at the Royal Hotel, or later at the Park Hotel, or still later in his own restaurant. After rising to the level of first chef at both hotels he went to work at the Bamboo Restaurant. He subsequently bought out its owner and changed the name to Mario's Bamboo Restaurant.

Until he owned his own restaurant the only time I saw my father was on Sundays. He wasn't very strict with me but being from Badia Polesine he was a man of principles and one of them was that, "Once Italian, always Italian." I felt more Welsh than Italian by the time I was 12, and for most of my teenage years we had heated discussions about my "modern" ways. In 1961 when I was 14 I made the big mistake of telling him that I had cheered for England in its 3–2 win over Italy. I had never seen him so angry about anything. He lunged for me yelling, "You traitor!

You're Italian, not English!" An iron worker most of his life, my father was built like a weightlifter, and I could see it was not the right time to discuss my nationality. I raced to the toilet and locked myself in before he could catch me. My mother had been trying to calm him but by now his frustration at not being able to get hold of me had converted his anger into a seething rage and Mother was helpless. As for me I refused to come out of my hiding place for over four hours, when he finally promised my mother that he wouldn't attack me.

Dad made a big success of his restaurant. We all pitched in to help and, instead of soccer games or trips to the local movies with my friends, my evenings were spent washing mountains of sauce-stained dishes. And since I was so tall for my age, Dad put me to work as a waiter whenever the pile of dirty dishes disappeared.

Quite often I wouldn't get to bed until two in the morning, which meant my lack of sleep had to be made up somewhere. So what better place than school? Unfortunately, my relations with the teachers at Lady Mary's Grammar School were tumultuous, even when I was still getting eight hours' sleep at night. Now with only four or five hours (depending on how early Dad decided he needed potatoes peeled) I was more easily excited than ever, especially when awakened from a deep nap in the back row.

My mother claims I was the only pupil who came home from school bloodied from fistfights with teachers. For a long time she believed my explanations that I had fallen down in the playground every time I came home with battlescars. Then one day, after I had pulled the wig off my music teacher's head and wrestled him onto the floor (while thirty kids cheered me on), my mother had to face the not so nice truth about her son's classroom behavior.

We were both summoned to the headmaster's study

where the irate principal enumerated my faults at length. My mother gasped when she was told that seldom did a day pass in which I wasn't physically punished by one of the teachers. Like all mothers, though, she was still hopeful that my wild behavior had some justification.

"But why did you fight Mr. Robson?" she asked as the bandaged music teacher glared at me.

"Because he doesn't like me," I replied quickly.

"That's absurd!" interjected Mr. Robson.

"But why doesn't he like you?" my mother continued, ignoring his remark.

"Because I always say what I think."

So, you see, speaking my mind has always gotten me into trouble.

I probably wouldn't have been such a disruptive pupil if I had gone to one of today's modern American schools where students are encouraged to join in class discussion or interrupt teachers to argue a point. In Britain in the late fifties, teachers did most of the talking and class participation was limited to asking teachers questions in humble and subservient whispers. Well, I never felt humble or subservient, and whenever a teacher made a statement that I knew was inaccurate or prejudicial I was quick to let him know I disagreed.

These class interruptions usually led to my being marched to the front of the class for a good caning. Three whacks was the customary dosage but some more energetic teachers delighted in giving me up to ten. One teacher, a skinny little sadist, used to count out the number of blows as if he were refereeing a boxing match.

Looking back at my school days I realize now that I wasn't a bad student at all, just a rebel. Many times I was threatened with suspension or expulsion, but my soccer and track coaches could always be counted on to calm the headmaster down. I was, after all, the biggest boy in the school and in all modesty the star of the soccer and track teams. Because of this nonacademic clout I was even able to ignore the most sacred of Lady Mary's traditions, the wearing of the school uniform.

My favorite apparel was the rock-and-roll groups' uniform: drainpipe blue jeans and a black T shirt, topped off, of course, by a DA haircut. It was all too much for the headmaster and one evening he attempted to shame me into conforming. It was after I had appeared in the school play, a pretty mediocre production of *Henry the Third,* that he made his little speech. My mother and sister, listening raptly to his well chosen words, were startled when I became his subject. "There is a boy who is out to disrupt our way of life here at Lady Mary's," he said. "I think I should warn all you parents that he is a bad influence on our other pupils. While others willingly abide by the school rules he wears blue jeans to class."

Upon hearing the words "blue jeans," my sister and mother cringed with embarrassment. The faces that turned to stare at them didn't show their usual friendliness.

When I got home that night I had to promise my mother I would wear the school uniform the next day. However, within a week I was back to my casual gear; after all, I was not only captain of the soccer team but also the record holder of the javelin throw, the 100-yard dash, and the discus throw. With such credentials how could a pupil not be forgiven in sports-crazy Lady Mary's?

My powerful allies in the sports department were not always so high on me. In fact, at one time I thought the rugby coach was going to kill me. It happened when I first came to the school. I had transferred to Lady Mary's at the age of 11 from St. Peters, a school that only played rugby. The sports teacher there had written to the rugby coach at Lady Mary's to inform him that I had been the vice captain and a star of the team. He also mentioned that because of my size I could do well on the Lady Mary's team even though the school participated in an under-15-year-old league.

As soon as I registered at Lady Mary's an overweight bull of a man approached me in the school office and introduced himself. I can't remember his name now but we all called him Goliath—jeez, was he big!

"I hear you're a good rugby player," he said in a lilting Welsh accent. "So you'll be on my team if you do well in the tryouts."

"But I hear they have a soccer team here," I replied, and with my usual bluntness added, "I like soccer more."

"Soccer!" I can still see his wide nostrils dilating with disgust. "You're not playing soccer here. You're playing a man's game while you're at Lady Mary's: rugby."

For once I controlled my tongue and walked away nodding my head. When I told my father about the conversation, his reaction was true to form: "Rugby! What type of game is that for an Italian boy? You're going to play soccer."

Usually, Dad didn't get involved with school matters (that was Mother's department), but next morning he went to see the rugby coach. "My son is not going to play rugby. My family has never played rugby and we don't intend to."

Later that morning I saw the rugby coach in the playground. He yelled at me across the asphalt, "Had to run home and tell Daddy, eh, Chinaglia. Well, you had better be at tryouts Saturday."

That night my father told me to ignore the coach and go to the soccer tryouts. I did go to the soccer tryouts but it was a nerve-racking week for an 11-year-old as I had to avoid running into the rugby coach. The following Friday I was delighted to see my name on the sports bulletin board as one of those who had made the school soccer team. I was the only player who was 11. I felt extremely proud but my pleasure was short-lived, for further down the bulletin board I saw the name Chinaglia listed as a member of the school's rugby team also. And just to make life even more complicated I read that both teams had games scheduled for the following Saturday at the same time and on adjoining fields. Who said the life of a school jock is all glamor and fun?

The day before the games I received telephone calls from both coaches. The soccer coach was the newest addition to the teaching staff and I could tell from the way he talked that he was in awe of the big beefy rugby coach. His "You know, Chinaglia, if you prefer to play rugby I would not object" left me unsettled.

His colleague was slightly more emphatic. "Okay, no more mucking about, Chinaglia. Be at the field at nine tomorrow."

I really didn't know what to do. I loved soccer and wanted to play on the team but was fearful of the consequences if I did. I changed my mind at least four times on the way to the sports field that Saturday morning. At zero hour, with both coaches watching from their respective fields, I walked over to the soccer team and put on the school jersey. It was undoubtedly one of the most courageous and sensible decisions of my life. If I had played rugby in my school years I probably would have stayed with it, and even though it is a splendid game rugby could never have afforded me the lucrative career and wonderful life soccer has given me. Most of the fine rugby players I knew in Wales are still working in the Welsh coal mines.

I scored all three goals in our school's 3–0 victory that day and, despite acquiring a snarling enemy for the rest of my stay at Lady Mary's, I was never again badgered about playing on the rugby team.

Goals came easily for me while I was on both Lady Mary's and the Cardiff Schools all-star teams. In one game

I scored eight, another time 10 while playing in the under-15 division.

When I was almost 15 I became aware of the scouts from the professional teams at the Cardiff Schools' team matches. We soon got to know who they were and which teams they represented. Cardiff City, Swansea Town, Wrexham, Bristol City, and Bristol Rovers were the ones most interested in the likely prospects on our team.

For years I had dreamed of playing for Cardiff City, the most famous of all Welsh clubs, which had just dropped down from the first division. So I was beside myself with joy when a scout from that club came to our apartment to talk to my father about my playing for the club. "Of course, Giorgio will have to come to the club for a trial game so we can take a look at him," he added after describing the opportunities awaiting any boy who was lucky enough to play for Cardiff.

I know I shocked him when I said I couldn't come for a tryout. I thought it ridiculous when all the Cardiff Schools' games were played at Cardiff City's own Ninian Park Stadium.

"If you want to see me play," I remember telling him, "then watch me when we play Wrexham Schools at Ninian Park."

I saw the scout sitting in the stands the day we played the Wrexham all-star team. We won 5–0 and I scored a hat trick. After the game when he came over to congratulate me I figured I was already a Cardiff player. But instead he said, "You played well, like a pro, Giorgio, but if you want to play for Cardiff City you've still got to come back here for a trial."

I was stunned. It didn't seem possible after the tremendous game I had had that he wanted to take another look at me. As much as I wanted to play for Cardiff, I was too independent to accept his condition so I told him I had no intention of trying out for Cardiff City. He left me shrugging his shoulders, and the bewildered expression on his face suggested he thought I was crazy.

Another man who had watched the game was Walter Robbins, coach of the Swansea Town club, a second-division squad not as fashionable as Cardiff or with such a proud history. Robbins, however, was more to my taste. He said he wanted to sign me up as an apprentice professional right away. No trial, just a few signatures. I said yes immediately and took him home to see my father. Within two weeks I had begun my professional career.

At least I was on the road to professionalism. During the summer months I went through what so many thousands of other eager young British players have gone through before me: a period of endless chores, like sweeping the stands, cleaning the players' boots (now called shoes), cutting the grass, washing the dressing room floors, scrubbing out the shower stalls, and whatever else could be done by unskilled teenage hands. It was hard and absolutely the most boring work, but every one of the seven apprentices at the club was happy to put up with those many grueling hours in exchange for the few afternoons each week when we were permitted to train with the team players.

My dreams of stardom never materialized at Swansea, although I did play for the first team once when only 15½. Unfortunately, I don't think I touched the ball more than twice during the entire game. The only reason they put me in was because of the extensive injuries the club had suffered the previous week. So I got my chance to move up from the reserve team, away from the teenage apprentices and aging veterans, to face some of the best pros in the second division of the English Football League. It was a Football League Cup match with Rotherham in the north of England, and I was thankful the Swansea fans didn't see the game. We won, but not because of anything I contributed.

It was over a year before club manager Trevor Morris gave me another chance on the first team. This time it was a regular league game at home against Portsmouth, one of the top teams in England in the 1940s and 1950s when it won the first-division championship twice. Marking me that afternoon at center back was Jimmy Dickinson, Portsmouth's long-serving captain. He was probably the best midfielder in England during his younger days, but had by this time switched to defense as many veteran midfielders do. He was more than twice my age but no one would have ever guessed it from the way he kept me bottled up in the penalty area. I saw less of the ball than I did against Rotherham. It certainly was not the kind of home debut I had been dreaming about for over eighteen months. I'm sure that if any of the Swansea Town fans had been told that afternoon that my biggest goal in life was to become another goalscoring striker like Bobby Charlton, my soccer idol, the laughter would have been heard in Cardiff, over forty miles away.

I only played in six games for the first team in the four years I was with Swansea even though I was the top scorer on the reserve team. Manager Trevor Morris didn't think much of me, nor did his successor, Glen Davis. The only one on the club who thought I had a future was Ivor Allchurch, the famous Welsh star who was a legend in Wales. Ivor played a record 68 times for the Welsh national team and was considered the best inside forward in Britain during the 1950s. When I was seventeen and being fined weekly by the management for some infraction or other it was Ivor who lifted my sagging spirits by telling me, "One day, Giorgio, you're going to be as famous as Bobby Charlton."

"You're just trying to be nice," I replied.

"No, I mean it, Giorgio. You've got the skill and what's more important the right mentality for top soccer."

I often thought of Ivor's kind words, especially when I had real doubts that I would ever make it into top soccer. He has probably never known just how important an impact his interest and kind words had on that uncertain teenager. Ivor taught me something I have never forgotten: that the older established players have a duty to give a helping hand to all the youngsters on the team.

If there ever was a youngster who needed help it was me. Because of the fines imposed upon me I was always hungry and at this late date I would like to apologize to all those trusting Swansea housewives who left their milk outside their front doors after the milkman had made his rounds. Without that free supply of nourishing milk I would never have made it.

I suppose it was partly my independent streak again but as hungry as I was I didn't feel I could tell my parents about my financial situation. What I did do, however, was insist that my mother visit me every weekend so that she could take me out to eat.

For a teenager over six feet tall and weighing about 170 I did not have a big appetite. Consequently, my mother was quick to remark that my eating habits had changed drastically when every time we finished a meal in a restaurant I would say, "Do you mind if I have the same again, Mum?"

Another way I managed to keep going without sixpence to my name was to depend on the generosity of three Italian ice cream peddlers. Whenever I would see their carts parked on a street corner, I knew I would be offered as many ice creams as I could consume for they always thought I looked too thin.

When I was 19 Glen Davis, the manager then, gave me a free transfer (similar to becoming a free agent). The directors of the club asked him why he would let a promising young center forward who was scoring goals leave without trying to get a transfer fee from some other club, and his reply was, "Because he's never going to make it in professional soccer."

I think that Davis did me a great service when he let me go. My father had already arranged for me to sign with a third-division team in Italy, Massese, but I wanted to stay in British soccer and I am certain that if Swansea had placed me on the transfer list a British club would have paid the necessary amount for my transfer. Now there was little hope of a British career for a free transfer stigmatizes a person. Coaches (often mistakenly) assume that a released player is worthless, either because he has reached the veteran stage of his career or, as in my case, because he is a youngster who couldn't make the grade.

When my father insisted I took a week's holiday to visit Massese, which is in the town of Massa. Since Massa is Carrara's neighbor, I was able to stay with my grandmother and relatives while taking a good look at what I might be getting into. I was not all that thrilled about starting in a new league and even less about adjusting to a new environment. Even though I was an Italian I had become very Anglicized. I was visibly a member of the British youth culture of the sixties and provoked many comments and stares from the people of Massa with my long velvet jacket, tight drainpipe pants, heavy shoes, and long Beatles haircut.

The Massese club officials must have sensed that I was not anxious to live in Italy again because on the day I was to return to Wales they presented me with a brand-new Fiat sports car. Even now, I can't describe the effect that gleaming beauty had on me. I had been earning about $40 a week at Swansea and here was a club casually offering me a $4,000 automobile as a perk. It was its dollar value, not the car itself, that impressed me so. Here at last was a sign that I could actually close a door on my poverty-stricken youth. As much as I loved soccer, the main reason I had been so determined to succeed in the game was that I desperately needed the financial security I had never known. All of a sudden the Massese club seemed to be the pot of gold at the end of the rainbow. *Giorgio,* I said to myself, *this is goodbye to fish and chips and warm beer.*

Upon arriving back in Swansea I learned that Cardiff City was interested in me, but by this time the dollar signs were in my eyes and I couldn't wait to return to Italy. Moreover, my father hadn't wasted any time going back to Massese and arranging everything. I was to receive a monthly salary of $500 (plus $60 for every point the team earned) and my father, a bonus of $30,000—both incredible sums in British soccer at that time. The average salary for players in the English first division was around $12,000 a year, a comfortable salary no doubt in the mid-sixties, but paltry compared to the $30,000 to $40,000 average of the Italian first division.

I was soon to discover that in return for their generous compensation Italian soccer clubs expected their players to accept some infringements on their privacy and devote more time to club activities than their British counterparts did.

I arrived at Massese in June 1966. Within three days I discovered what was meant by the term "loss of privacy." For the first two days I stayed at my grandmother's house in Carrara, going to the beach daily and getting reacquainted with relatives and neighbors. In Britain summer is the off-season for soccer so I presumed I was in for a marvelous couple of months, what with my flashy little car and the fantastic girls parading up and down the golden Riviera beaches between Viareggio and Portofino. No one had bothered to mention that when the regular Italian season ends the Italian teams play exhibition games, enter various tournaments, such as the Alps Cup, and somehow manage to run off the entire Italian Cup tournament.

When the club secretary left a message at my grandmother's for me to pack enough clothes for three weeks, I thought at first it meant we were off on one of those pleasant summer tours teams took in the fifties and sixties in which sightseeing was more important to the players than the games played. Later I learned the team was only going as far as Castelnuovo di Garfag, a nearby mountain resort for *ritiro* (an intensive training camp in which the players are completely isolated).

Of all the adjustments I had to make upon entering Italian soccer the toughest for me was to get used to *ritiro*. Hard physical training, strict dieting, and bed checks at nine p.m. were enough to drive a typical healthy British teenager around the bend. At Swansea I had been accustomed to coming home at all hours of the night and going to practice at ten in the morning and going home again either at twelve or four. Spending the rest of the day and most of the night having fun was my idea of how a teenager's life should be spent. Now I found myself in a prison-like atmosphere high in the Apuan Mountains with no social life at all. Worse yet, I was surrounded by a bunch of simple farmer types who considered me a comically dressed foreigner. They were nice enough but so far removed from my Beatles-inspired world that they probably thought the Rolling Stones had something to do with a landslide.

I felt like a complete outsider at the camp and to make matters worse homesickness for Wales hit me like a brick. One night while my new teammates were asleep I packed my case and left. The club officials discovered I was gone the next morning. At first they thought my leaving was a practical joke because they had never heard of a rookie soccer player leaving without permission. They telephoned my grandmother and asked to talk to me.

"He's already gone," she told them.

"Gone? Gone where?" they asked, hoping I was on my way back to the camp.

My grandmother's reply was very clear. "To Cardiff," she said.

CHAPTER 2

ONE THING I HADN'T EXPECTED on Giorgio's Day was Jim Karvellas' announcement to the crowd that the Cosmos had arranged a big surprise for me: a group of Italians had been flown in from Rome.

Believe me, my mouth was agape when onto the field rolled an electric cart carrying the widow and four children of my former coach Tommaso Maestrelli, who had died of cancer in 1976. For those of you who believe I'm hardhearted, let me tell you that I cried like a baby upon embracing my second family.

As my wife, Connie, can tell you, I spent more time at the Maestrellis' than I did at home during those wonderful years when Tommaso was coaching Lazio. His death at the height of his career was a tragic loss to both his family and friends and also to Italian soccer. His kindness and understanding left a deep impression on all those fortunate enough to have had their lives touched by him. I think he was the wisest and sincerest man I have ever met. I loved him like his own sons did and to see his family so unexpectedly in the middle of Giants Stadium brought back many poignant memories.

Mrs. Maestrelli whispered to me that she and her four children were going to stay in New York for three days. Elated at the prospect of showing them the wonderful sights of the city, I ran off the field to rejoin my teammates for the start of the day's game.

Tulsa was the visiting team, a squad that included eight former English first-division players. Tulsa had started the season strong, winning its first four games, but had leveled off to a 5–3 record by the time they arrived at Giants Stadium. Although the Cosmos had not been playing well in 1979 no one on our team was especially worried about meeting Tulsa on our home field even though Franz Beckenbauer was unavailable. Franz had been out since our April 22 game with Fort Lauderdale. He, along with Werner Roth, Eskandarian, Seninho, Dennis Tueart, Carlos Alberto, and Boris Bandov, had made our dressing room look like an army field hospital of late. The loss of so many of our star performers was obviously the major reason for our uninspiring performances so far, but with a quarter of the season gone and the injury list expanding weekly it seemed very important that we learn to play with what we had as well as develop a more forceful and rhythmic style.

At the beginning of the season all of us at the Cosmos were confident that at last we would have a world-class team with the addition of the brilliant and explosive Brazilian World Cup genius Marinho; the Iranian international defender Eskandarian; and the strong and creative midfielder from Argentina, Antonio Carbognani; as well as the likely prospect of Johan Neeskens, the world's best midfielder from Holland, joining us before the summer. As the season progressed it rapidly became clear, however, to both the front office and the playing staff, that we had some real problems. Some pundits thought we had too many stars for a well balanced team to emerge; others said we failed because our players squabbled too often; another school of thought pointed out that we couldn't possibly win all the time as the other NASL teams were improving at a rapid rate.

I didn't think our failures were due to any of these reasons. From my vantage point as interim captain and one of our more experienced players (along with Carlos Alberto and Franz Beckenbauer), I could see that what was missing in our makeup was a fierce dedication to training and a determination in actual match play. Too many of our players were beginning to believe that just because we had beaten all our competition and won the last two NASL championships we were automatically going to win in 1979, even if we didn't exert ourselves in the majority of games.

Four or five years ago, a team comprising such stars as the Cosmos now field might have overwhelmed all its opposition in the NASL. But in today's NASL there is an abundance of fine experienced players, including many former World Cup stars, as well as a host of topnotch coaches. Teams of the proven caliber of Tampa Bay, Vancouver, Chicago, Fort Lauderdale, and Minnesota, just to name a few, can compete with teams in any country. And whenever you face a coach with the proven reputation of a Rinus Michels (Los Angeles), Gordon Jago (Tampa Bay), Tony Waiters (Vancouver), Noel Cantwell (New England), or Hubert Vogelsinger (San Diego) you know your team will be tested both tactically and strategically, regardless of which players line up against you.

Our first game in 1979 pitted us against Vogelsinger's tough San Diego Sockers, a team filled with hard-running Europeans. Hubert has the knack of getting the best out of his players, particularly when they play the Cosmos. He is a strict disciplinarian and no one stays long with him unless he can run 90 minutes nonstop; Austrian-born Hubert probably has the toughest training program of any NASL coach.

It was clear within the first few minutes that the 1979

Sockers were in better physical condition than ever. Before a record home crowd of 16,396 the Sockers, making good use of their fast wingers Jean Willrich and Ade Coker, outran us in the first half. We were hard pressed and failed to take control of the midfield like we usually did. Yet we led, 1–0, at halftime as a result of a killer pass by Vladislav Bogicevic that split the Sockers' defense, enabling me to find room to shoot and score.

In the second half the Sockers earned their well deserved equalizer in the 46th minute when Ade Coker headed a ball past Erol Yasin in goal. After that goal we began to improve, especially after Francisco Marinho came on as a sub in the 65th minute. But the final whistle blew with the game still tied, 1–1, although the Sockers had a goal disallowed on an offside call only two minutes before the end.

In the NASL a tie is treated differently from the way it is in the rest of the world. Instead of earning one point apiece and a well deserved rest, we had to return to the field for more action.

The NASL has tampered with the century-old rules of soccer for a good reason. Defensive-minded teams that are content to earn no more than one point when playing away from home have turned off the fans all over the world. To insure that teams don't stonewall for 90 minutes and can't play for a 0–0 result, the NASL has eliminated the tie game. Instead the league awards six points for a win (traditionally it's two), bonus points for goals scored, and an overtime period whenever a game is tied at the end of regulation time. Probably the NASL's most controversial innovation is the one used to decide the winner if overtime fails: the shootout (a series of penalty kicks with the goalie permitted to go off his line to confront the kicker).

Although these changes in the rules have been met with cries of horror throughout the 145 countries that are a part of international organized soccer, I think the NASL was right in thinking they would help make American soccer more attractive to new fans. However, I would like to see some consideration given to reverting to the international rules once soccer is fully established as a major sport here.

At San Diego we didn't have to resort to a shootout since Seninho scored a spectacular goal from 25 yards out in the eighth minute of overtime.

Winning the first game of the season and doing it on the road gives a boost to any team, and we all hoped that our victory might inspire us to play up to our potential. But I thought our next performances were even weaker.

Some of my friends feel I expect too much from the Cosmos. The day before the Tulsa game on "Giorgio's Day" they said, "Giorgio, your team is seven and one; it's clear the Cosmos will win your division; you're the leading goalscorer; what else do you want?"

I suppose I take soccer and the Cosmos so seriously because of a well developed sense of pride. I've always had an intense desire to make any team I belong to the very best. Now the Cosmos are my home and naturally I want them to be *the* team. Soccer has always been more than just a sport or a job to me and, unlike many players I know, I could never sweep soccer to the back of my mind when I go home at night. Only my family rivals it for my love and devotion. My friends call me a bigamist, married to both my family and soccer. Probably I am.

Because I myself am so serious about soccer, I am appalled when other players or teammates take the game lightly. In my opinion it's a rare privilege to be earning a living playing the world's greatest sport. I can't think of any other occupation like the professional athlete's. He gets paid so well for doing something he would do anyway even if he wasn't being paid. And yet there are many professionals who show up for training and sometimes even for games feeling lousy from eating or drinking too much.

I wish dedication were transferable. But all I can do when I see my teammates not trying hard enough is to let them know how I feel. As interim captain in 1979 I didn't hesitate to let my Cosmos teammates know how annoyed I was by their performance in those first eight games. The more frustrated I got at seeing so many fine players wasting their talent the more I yelled at the team. By the middle of May I was constantly complaining on the field.

On Giorgio's Day I nervously prepared to face Tulsa, a squad that was capable of giving us a real test. It was a very experienced team that would take advantage of any mistakes we might make. The Roughnecks employed a crisp 4–3–3 system with depth in defense, a powerful midfield, and a fast buildup in their attack whenever they switched from defense. Able to field eight former English first-division players, including three from the Derby County team that won the English championship in 1975 (in goalie Colin Boulton, defender David Nish, and midfielder Steve Powell), Tulsa had the wherewithal to give us a good game.

When the teams lined up to be introduced the crowd of 46,000 gave a warm welcome to each member of the visiting team: Colin Boulton (goalkeeper); Terry Darracott, Don O'Riordan, Sammy Chapman, and Greg Ryan (defenders); Steve Powell, David Nish, and Iraj Danaifard (midfielders); and Alan Woodward, Bill Sautter, and Lawrie Abrahams (strikers).

And then came the Cosmos.

Jack Brand, the agile and safe goalkeeper replacing Turkish international Erol Yasin, was playing his first game of the season. Jack, a former Toronto and Rochester star, had spent most of his time since coming to the Cosmos in 1978 fighting for Erol's spot. Coach Eddie

Firmani had not been pleased with Erol's performance the previous week against Tampa Bay but had not informed Erol of his decision to play Jack until a few hours before kickoff time. Erol was furious and argued with Eddie against the decision. Maybe he shouldn't have been so surprised at being dropped but I can understand his anger.

Their arguing was nothing out of the ordinary. For the last three years filling the goalkeeper position has been a constant source of friction between Cosmos goalkeepers and coaches. Erol argued with Gordon Bradley when he and Shep Messing competed for the spot in 1977, as well as with Eddie in 1978 over the 10 games Jack played. Now it looked as if the goalies were to seesaw up and down again.

Another goalkeeper on the Cosmos staff was our 22-year-old U.S. international Dave Brcic. Of the three goalkeepers I have a preference for Erol. He has that all-important attribute of being able to rise to the occasion, and the more important the game the better he plays. But I must say that, like many others around the Cosmos camp, I believe that young Dave Brcic will blossom into the best goalkeeper in the country within a few years.

At right back was that ball of fire Bobby Smith, probably the most courageous and fearless defender anywhere and certainly one of the best defenders yet produced in U.S. soccer. However, Bobby has a serious drawback: his aggressiveness often gets him into trouble with the referee.

Scheduled to play sweeper on the team was Carlos Alberto, the ultimate exponent of ball control, with an unflappable defensive style. No one who has seen this inimitable Brazilian superstar sweep the ball off an onrushing opponent's foot with a gentle flick will ever forget him. He makes his difficult defensive position look downright easy. And the sly way he moves up into the attack is a delight to watch. All in all, I'm his biggest fan—except when I lose to him at poker.

Another player who didn't have to worry about losing his spot on the team was our center back, Wim Rijsbergen, our new Dutch import. Like Carlos, Wim (pronounced Vim) is a famous World Cup star, great at mopping up opponents' attacking sorties. He's also extremely fast with the ball and willing to run nonstop throughout a game. A quiet thoughtful type, Wim is a true gentleman of the old school and you'd never suspect he's such a tenacious battler on the field if you saw him curled up with his books on our road trips.

A noticeable absentee from our lineup on my big day was Werner Roth, our club captain and longest-serving member, who was still recovering from a knee injury. Werner has been a standout center back ever since he first put on a Cosmos shirt in 1972. He is the only man in the NASL to have won three championship medals, and I knew he was anxious to get back into training so as not to miss out on the action for the fourth (fingers crossed), come Soccer Bowl 1979. (It was not to be, of course.)

Standing next to Wim Rijsbergen would be Santiago Formoso, who had been holding down the left back position since Iranian World Cup defender Andranik Eskandarian fractured his cheekbone in an earlier game. Santiago, who played for Hartford and Connecticut, is also a U.S. international. An exceptionally good tackler with amazing speed, Santiago had some great games for the Cosmos in 1978. But with the coming of Eskandarian, he would have to be in top form every game to keep his place on the team.

I mention these and other rivalries only to show the stunning strength of the Cosmos bench in 1979. Few other NASL teams could play with any consistency after losing four regular members.

Occupying the right midfield position for the Tulsa game would be another of the Cosmos' world-class players, Francisco Marinho. Francisco made his mark as a

defender for the Brazilian national team but was now ply-
ing his magic out of midfield where his amazing ball control, acceleration, and thundering shot could be utilized
more. His arrival and that of Johan Neeskens, scheduled
for a month later, would give us the best midfield of any
team in the world. For not only was Vladislav Bogicevic
(or Bogie to everyone), the brilliant Yugoslavian international, still playing top-class soccer, but there was also the
incomparable Emperor Franz sitting on the touchlines
with a sprained knee.

Marinho, Neeskens, Bogicevic, and Beckenbauer—I,
along with thousands of others in the New Jersey area,
couldn't wait to see those four artists on the Giants Stadium turf together. But for the Tulsa game it was going
to be Marinho, Bogie, and young Ricky Davis, perhaps the
most remarkable of all three, for here was a 21-year-old
American firmly established on a team of world stars and
improving with each game.

We had an overabundance of talent, all right, for we
had other top-class and experienced midfielders on the
club roster. For one there was Terry Garbett, master of
defensive midfield and an excellent passer, who next to
Werner Roth was our longest-serving player. Unlucky,
with numerous injuries, Terry played only 15 games in
1978 and was also hurt for much of 1979. Another fine midfielder waiting in the wings that afternoon was Boris
Bandov, yet another U.S. international in the Cosmos sta-
ble of fine young American talent. Boris is a powerful player with a tendency to go forward and get among the goalscorers. Antonio Carbognani is another midfielder who
likes to shoot for goal. A former Argentinian first-division
player, Antonio is endowed with that fine technique and
skill we've come to expect from Argentinians. Apart from
a nine-minute stint in one game, Antonio had not yet had
a chance to show his talent since joining us in the winter.

The three forwards for the Tulsa game would be

Dennis Tueart, myself, and Mark Liveric. Dennis was one of the best wingers in Europe when he came to the Cosmos in 1978. The left winger on the English national team, he plays on either wing with us and quite often moves into the middle to strike for goal. He has a tremendous shot, controls the ball brilliantly, and runs like a greyhound. He is a gamewinner if there ever was one, probably the most dangerous forward in the NASL when the ball is at his feet in the opponents' penalty area.

On the other wing would be Mark Liveric, a Cosmos player in 1974–75 and only recently returned to the club from Edmonton. He had also played at San Jose, Washington, and Oakland since leaving the Cosmos. A muscular yet speedy winger, Mark was taking the injured Seninho's place.

Seninho, the Portuguese international, is another of those Latin players who makes difficult tasks seem simple. Although a marvelous dribbler, he is usually a direct player who uses his great speed to glide past opponents.

One other winger not starting was Gary Etherington, the 21-year-old U.S. international. A likable and happy youngster, Gary trains very hard and is the type whose motivation and drive insure success. If he continues to improve as he has I expect him to become the premier American forward of the 1980s.

After the teams had been presented, Tulsa's captain, Terry Darracott, a fine defender from the Everton club of England, and I watched referee Peter Johnson flip the coin. Terry won and he elected to kick with the sun behind him. There wasn't much sun to be seen but occasionally it was breaking through the low-lying clouds to brighten up the stadium.

I was very disappointed with the weather: a heavy rain all day Saturday and forecasts for rain all day Sunday had kept the crowd down to less than 50,000. We had been hoping for a 60,000 turnout, for anything less is no longer considered a big attendance for the Cosmos.

In the first few minutes, Tulsa sent a series of long balls upfield to its strikers Lawrie Abrahams and the young American Bill Sautter. The Roughnecks were testing our defenders and they very nearly scored. David Nish, the English international, caught the left side of our defense napping with a beautiful through pass to Lawrie Abrahams. Accelerating with a tremendous burst of speed, Abrahams went past Bobby Smith then crossed the ball to Woodward who came close with a low zooming shot that whizzed past the near post.

In the fourth minute another long ball went to Abrahams. This time Bobby Smith tripped him in the penalty area and referee Johnson pointed immediately to the penalty spot. Terry Barracott scored with a fierce shot into the right-hand corner and we were down, 1–0.

Here we go again, I thought. Another game in which we would have to fight from behind. I'm from the old school; I like to be winning in the early stages of a game. The popular belief that trailing by a goal brings out the best in a team may often be true but it can also cause a team to get overanxious, desperate, and even foolish. I've seen too many losing teams leave themselves wide open in the back when throwing everything into the attack for an equalizer.

On this occasion, however, we were lucky because the Tulsa goal had a positive effect: it motivated us to put more effort into our game. Within a minute of Darracott's goal, Bogie sent a ground ball out to Dennis on the left wing. Dennis cut in toward goal, avoided a tackle from Don O'Riordan, then, as he was about to shoot, was pushed off the ball by two defenders. Referee Johnson ignored the infraction and waved play on. What looked like a certain goal came to nothing. It was a terrible decision—one of the many outrageous calls to be made by Johnson during the game. Although I thought I had grown accustomed to the frequently inept and amateurish officiating in the NASL, I was astonished by the refereeing Johnson did for that Tulsa game.

I felt happier about our chances after seeing how easily Dennis had moved into scoring position before he was brought down. That sixth sense of soccer players told me we would be scoring before the day was over. (Dennis, in fact, had a marvelous game, moving beautifully and tormenting the Tulsa defense all afternoon.) In the 17th minute Dennis equalized for us following some brilliant passing between Santiago Formoso and Mark Liveric on the left wing.

Until that goal I must confess I was shocked with the way most of us were playing. Our defense seemed shaky, especially anytime our defenders saw Alan Woodward and Lawrie Abrahams advancing with the ball; our midfield was not running off the ball enough and up front Dennis and Francisco, although doing brilliant things with the ball, were continually running toward me in the penalty area bringing their markers with them and bottling me up near goal. But after Dennis' tying goal we began to click and for 25 minutes we looked like world beaters.

In the back of our defense Carlos was picking off the Tulsa attackers as they raced for their long balls and flipping difficult balls gently over their heads to either Bobby, Wim, or Santiago. After receiving the return passes Carlos would join our midfielders in pretty one-touch passing right up to the Tulsa penalty area. On one occasion Carlos was near his own goal line when he lofted a ball over Woodward's head to Santiago, and he in turn hit it while it was still waist high over the head of Powell to Bogie who did the same trick to yet another opponent. Liveric joined in the ping-pong-like action and the ball was passed between them all the way to the other goal line

with the ball never touching the ground once. It was a remarkable exhibition of skill seldom seen outside of
Brazilian soccer, and the crowd roared its approval.

In the 32nd minute Carlos, again attacking from his
sweeper position, dribbled past two defenders just outside
the right side of the Tulsa penalty area. When Tulsa's big
center back Sammy Chapman came in to tackle, he
flicked the ball to Dennis who had only goalkeeper Boulton to beat. Dennis faked going to the left, then dribbled
to the right leaving Boulton on the ground clutching grass.
Dennis now faced an open goal but instead of pushing the
ball in he tapped it to me for what was an obvious Giorgio's Day present. I must admit I love to score goals—even
gift goals like the one Dennis provided me with so un-
selfishly. For two or three seconds I soar into space with
ecstasy, not knowing what I'm doing or saying. I get so
excited I have no way of controlling it and I suppose
many fans, particularly those of opposing teaams, must feel
I'm some kind of fringe lunatic. When I came back to
earth again, I was lifting Dennis off his feet in a bear hug
while other teammates were hugging and kissing me.

I know there are many who dislike it when we players
get so demonstrative. When I was a kid the pros simply
shook hands after a goal and walked back to the center
circle. To hug or kiss another player was considered (to
put it mildly) a sissy thing to do. Well, I prefer by far
the modern style where emotions are not shackled. It's
wonderful when affection and happiness can flow freely.

I was very pleased by the tremendous cheering that
greeted my goal. All professional athletes love adulation;
I'm the first to admit to an unquenchable thirst for approval and applause. The cheering after that goal was even
more gratifying since I felt it was more for me than for
the goal, which as I have said really belonged to Dennis.
(Incidentally, for some inexplicable reason, the Boo
Chinaglia Club join in the cheering whenever I score.)

We kept up our nonstop attack on the Tulsa goal and were rewarded with another goal four minutes later. Then Sammy Chapman tripped me as I was sprinting into the penalty area. A penalty!

I'm the one who takes the Cosmos' penalty kicks and normally before a game I've learned something about the opposing goalkeeper's method of facing them. Some are weaker on low balls, some move slower to balls hit on their left sides, some have difficulties with curving balls going into the corner. Then, of course, there are some who have no apparent weaknesses.

Colin Boulton belongs to the last group. One of the most experienced goalies in the world, Colin knows exactly what to do in any given situation. The only way to beat him is to put the ball far enough away from his six-foot frame with such speed that he is unable to leap across the goal in one of his spectacular dives. I knew the ball had to go into one of the corners of the net.

Scoring from a penalty kick should be one of the simplest acts in soccer. Everything is in the kicker's favor: the ball is placed only 12 yards from the goal; there is a generous target of 24 feet by eight feet to aim at and, best of all, the goalie is not permitted to come off his line or move until the kick is taken. Theoretically, if the ball is kicked correctly, say a foot away from either post, a goalkeeper should never be able to see it until it's past him. And yet one out of every three penalties is either saved or, even worse, kicked over or past the posts. On Giorgio's Day I hoped this was not going to be the imperfect one of the three.

I aimed for the inside of the right post and was relieved to see the netting shake as the ball went in with some force.

We were now leading by two goals, and since we were so obviously dominating the play it was becoming a question of how many more we were going to score. We left the field at halftime extremely confident and as pleased at our performance as the cheering fans were.

There was another ceremony on the field during halftime. Ahmet Ertegun presented five high school students with Giorgio Chinaglia college scholarships. I spend a good deal of my free time involved in youth activities so this generous gesture was very satisfying for me. As Giorgio's Day progressed I was becoming happier by the hour. Rejoining my teammates as they streamed out on the field, I found it hard to believe that only an hour before I had been so upset by the booing.

Our luck unexpectedly fizzled out minutes after the restart. Bobby Smith, who in the first half had some difficulty controlling the elusive Lawrie Abrahams, tackled Terry Darracott, missed the ball and kicked Darracott's leg. Bobby's terrible temper is well known. Predictably, he defended his action to a group of Tulsa players while the referee checked to see how seriously injured Darracott was. I ran over and tried to get Bobby to move away but he continued to argue and then, just as I anticipated, the referee brought out a red card and flashed it in his face. Bobby's ejection left us with 10 men for the last 38 minutes of the match. It was no longer going to be a one-sided game.

Apart from one good shot by Marinho, we didn't come close to scoring for the rest of the game. Tulsa, on the other hand, looked dangerous on a number of occasions. We were lucky to withstand some heavy pressure in the last 15 minutes. Lawrie Abrahams failed to connect when only a few yards from the goal, and a shot from Alan Woodward went screaming past the outside of the upright with Jack Brand beaten. Then, with a few minutes remaining, Steve Earle, who had come on as a substitute, saw his great header saved on a magnificent flying dive by Jack.

We were relieved to hear the final whistle, yet we also

felt proud of how well we had fought to hold the Roughnecks to their first-half goal with only 10 men. Perhaps
the team was now ready to jell into the superteam we
had been expecting since the season's opener.

After the game there was a big reception in my honor in
the Giants Stadium clubhouse. Over five hundred guests
were downstairs in the clubhouse when I arrived. Connie
and my three children, Cynthia, George, and Stephanie,
were there, as were my parents, Connie's parents, the
Maestrellis, the Cosmos players, and most of the Cosmos
executives.

Among the other invited guests were friends from as far
afield as Rome, London, the Bahamas, and Los Angeles.
My friends are a warmhearted bunch. Sergio Valente, the
famous hairdresser to Italian and American movie stars, is
typical. He insisted he had come from Rome only to cut
my hair for the big day and planned to leave first thing in
the morning. Fortunately, before the evening was over I
had convinced him to stay a few days and see New York
with the Maestrellis and Connie and me.

It was a happy festive occasion as most of the guests took
advantage of the fine array of hot and cold delicacies,
imported wines and assorted spirits, all of which were provided by the Cosmos' management. I must say that with
our club money is no object, providing that the result is
first class.

During yet another ceremony Werner Roth presented
me with a beautiful plaque on behalf of the players and
Ahmet Ertegun followed with a huge trophy housing a
silver soccer ball. Some local soccer groups also presented
gifts and I was pleased that my manager, Peppe Pinton,
was in attendance to help me transport home all the splendid presents I had collected since early afternoon. One gift
that really impressed me was a superb portrait of myself
by Leroy Neiman; I have it hanging in my study now.

One blemish on what otherwise was a delightful evening

was the news that Phil Woosnam had been invited by the Cosmos to be one of the pregame dignitaries down on the field but had not participated even though he was at the game. Peppe, who is also my close friend in addition to being my business manager, was adamant in his belief that Woosnam's noninvolvement in my day spelled trouble for me: "He's snubbed you because he intends to make an example of you."

Peppe, who worries about me more than I do, had been warning me for weeks that Woosnam was on the warpath. As Peppe saw it, Woosnam was having his own problems with some dissatisfied club owners concerning his ineffectiveness and Peppe felt that Woosnam had to make a stand now to show everyone he was in command. I was beginning to agree with Peppe. Woosnam *was* carried away. Peppe had already explained to him that I had never said the things attributed to me in the story in *Sport* but Woosnam was not satisfied. He demanded that we get the author, David Hirshey, to go to his office and explain the quotes. As if we could force a first-class writer to go to his office! David, of course, refused and Woosnam was demanding a written apology.

My relationship with Woosnam has been a surprisingly disappointing one as far as I am concerned. Woosnam was one of the best midfielders in Britain during the late fifties and early sixties. Since he was a Welshman, I naturally was a fan of his when he was performing so well for the Welsh national team. I particularly remember the great game he had against England in 1961, a 1–1 tie. He and Ivor Allchurch and the legendary John Charles played their hearts out in a game Wales should have won. With my Welsh background, I assumed that Woosnam would be one man with whom I would quickly develop a close friendship when I came to the United States. Unfortunately, we never hit it off. To make matters worse, our relationship deteriorated after my request to get a

NASL franchise in Hartford was turned down. Perhaps my disappointment was misinterpreted by Woosnam as anger. In any case it's been obvious that he dislikes me. This impression was reinforced in the week prior to Giorgio's Day. The phone had been ringing constantly as various soccer enthusiasts were eager to congratulate me on my cover story in *Sports Illustrated*. Woosnam's call to Peppe, an extended complaint about the earlier *Sport* article, was in sharp contrast. No "well dones" from him. Peppe and I were both amazed that he could ignore such good coverage in America's most prestigious sports magazine. After all, it was bound to give U.S. soccer a boost.

Although I had not said anything that should make me feel guilty, my preoccupation with the Woosnam affair was affecting my conversation with friends as I sat in the Stadium Club. I was growing tense and when this happens I become reticent.

"Damned if I'm going to be morose tonight," I whispered to Connie as the party came to an end. "Let's go to Manhattan and hear some music."

We sent our children home with my sister Rita, who had come in from Cardiff for the week, and drove off to Elaine's. It may not be the most elegant night spot in New York but Elaine's is certainly one of the best places imaginable to meet nutty characters and famous personalities.

We didn't get home until four in the morning. By then I felt completely relaxed for, strange as it may seem, a late night out with good music, savory food, and a liberal supply of scotch (it has to be Chivas Regal) refreshes my mind just as a good training workout rejuvenates my body.

I've always been a night owl and it was for this very reason that I was reluctant to go back to Massese in 1966 after my abrupt departure following those intense training days so soon after my arrival from Wales. My father spent three days lecturing, coaxing, and at times swearing at me for acting like a child.

"I won't let you ruin your life," he said more than a few times during that fiery homecoming. "In Italy you can live like a king!"

I knew he was right but the horror of that mountain retreat was still too fresh in my memory for me to think logically. Dad had done everything he possibly could for me and I didn't really need reminding. Not only had he negotiated the terrific contract with Massese, but he had also forced the club to agree to selling me to a first-division club once my three-year mandatory stay in third division was completed. (One of the many complex rules in Italian soccer is the one that requires any player who has played in a foreign league to remain for a minimum of three years in the third division before being eligible to play in the first.)

After a few days I realized what a fool I had been to leave Italy. I admitted as much to my father and promised him I would never again allow my personal idiosyncracies to interfere with my soccer career. I took a plane to Genoa and reentered the monastic regimen of *ritiro*. I promised myself that I would be the model player, willing to accept whatever rules the club imposed. And I'm proud of the fact that I worked harder than anyone else for the next two weeks.

Believe it or not, in later years I came to be a firm believer in sending teams away for *ritiro*. It's a very sensible way of training soccer players, especially in a soccer-crazed country like Italy where players are thankful for the opportunity to get away from the fishbowl life of the big cities, the constant hounding by both friendly and unfriendly people, the worries and problems of everyday family life, and the gossipy and often malicious newspaper coverage of soccer personalities. You return from *ritiro* glowing physically and mentally stimulated. Even today I often move out of my house the day before a game (as I did for Giorgio's Day) and indulge myself in my own miniature version of *ritiro* in a nearby hotel where I empty my mind and concentrate on the coming game.

At Massese our team played *catenaccio,* the defensive system devised in Italy in the late fifties in which there are five or more defenders (including a sweeper). The few goals that are scored in the *catenaccio* system usually come about from speedy counterattacks. A goal a game is considered a small triumph, particularly away from home when a team is expected to defend for 90 minutes. At Swansea, on the other hand, we played 4–2–4, which is an offensive system and one in which the forwards (or strikers) often outnumber the defenders. In *catenaccio,* however, it is sometimes difficult to see the goal for the hordes of hard-tackling defenders in front of it. A center forward may get only one goalscoring opportunity during a game and if you want to succeed in Italy you have to make sure that each opportunity results in a goal.

I was built just right for *catenaccio.* Now six foot one and weighing 190 pounds, I was too big to be pushed around in the penalty area. The average Italian player is seldom taller than five foot ten and, apart from Giacinto Facchetti, the captain of both Inter-Milan and the Italian national team, I seldom met defenders as big as I was.

Although I scored in my first game with Massese—against my future club Lazio in a 2–2 exhibition game—I only scored a total of five goals in the 1966–67 league games. But I learned a lot that year, especially how to take care of myself in a crowded penalty area. We finished fourth and missed promotion to the second division by only a few points.

At the end of the season I was honored by being selected for the Italian under-21 team. In front of 20,000 fans in the northern city of Udinese, we beat the Austrian under-21 team, 2–1, and I scored the winning goal.

I didn't have much time to savor the sweetness of my double triumph—playing for Italy and scoring my first international goal—because the following day I was scheduled to report to the army to start my national service. I was not depressed at the prospect of eighteen months in military uniform. No, I wasn't mad. Far from it. You see, the Italian soccer federation (Federazione Italiana Giuoco Calcio) has this incredible agreement with the army. All professional players stayed together in a soccer regiment and not only were given time off to play for their clubs but also had all day to practice. Players from northern Italy were stationed in Bologna. The southerners were housed in Rome. This meant I would be spending the next eighteen months in Rome, an exciting city for anyone who is young, single, and has plenty of spending money.

Having a good time in Rome was not as easy as I had anticipated. The army had a firm rule (even for soccer players) that new recruits be confined to barracks for the first forty days. Thanks to my uncle in Carrara I found no difficulty in getting around that. He would park my Fiat outside the barracks wall and, à la Hollywood prison movies, I would quickly slide down the wall, jump into the car, and escape to freedom (though in my case it was usually a quick drive to one of the better restaurants in Rome, a city noted for its supreme cuisine).

Inevitably, I was caught. One night as I climbed back over the barracks wall I was seen by an officer in charge of my unit, a miserable bully whom all the recruits despised. He threatened to report me. I told him to drop dead. He pushed me against the wall, which was pretty foolish since he knew I was a tough customer. I managed to hit him a few times before I was arrested.

Even though I missed the nightlife of Rome, life in the army jail was restful. Most of my days were spent

lying on my bunk sleeping and whenever I felt the need
for some stimulation I would give a guard money to go
out and buy newspapers.

It was on one such peaceful morning that I received
quite a shock when my papers were delivered. The guard
carrying several Roman newspapers burst into my cell.
"Hey, Chinaglia, they've sold you to Internapoli," he
roared.

I scanned the headlines and began to cry. "CHINAGLIA
SOLD TO INTERNAPOLI FOR 100 MILLION LIRE."

It couldn't be true, I told myself. Massese had promised
that I would be going to Florence, one of the best teams
in the first division, once I finished my obligatory three
years in the third division. I didn't want to go to another
third-division team, even if it *was* willing to pay what
amounted to $180,000 for my transfer.

I cried for a long time that morning.

That afternoon, as I lay on my bunk wondering how I
could get out of moving to the Naples club, a sergeant
unlocked my cell door and said curtly, "Okay, Chinaglia,
let's go. You've got some bigshot visitors."

Outside in the courtyard three officials from Internapoli,
smiling warmly and arms outstretched, trotted toward me.

"Congratulations, Giorgio!" the first to reach me said
as he shook my hand.

"It's a big day for you," added the second.

The third man, clutching a sheaf of papers, was more
solemn. "We need these contracts signed before we return
to Naples."

"But where are the Massese people?" I asked defiantly.
"You might as well know right away that if no one is here
from my club I will not talk to any of you."

Having said that, I turned around and strode back to
my cell, leaving them standing in the courtyard, bewildered, for players were generally grateful to move to bigger and richer clubs. Within fifteen minutes the sergeant

stormed into my cell. "The colonel has ordered you to go back and talk to the gentlemen from Naples, and you'd better behave yourself this time, Chinaglia."

For our second meeting we were ushered into one of the prison offices where we all confronted each other around a long wooden table.

Before they had a chance to speak I got off my chest some of my annoyance about the underhanded way my future was being decided. I criticized them for not involving me in the negotiations and demanded to be told all the details of the transaction, particularly what they were offering me as compensation for leaving a team that had promised to sell me to Florence. "And furthermore," I announced at the conclusion of my tirade, "I'm starving to death. So if you want to talk to me go out and buy me a chicken and a bottle of good wine."

Delgaudio, the vice president of the club, flicked his head toward the door and Pichiteria, one of his assistants, disappeared in a flash. He was back in no time with two baked chickens, two bottles of Soave, and a tray of pastries. I can't remember anything ever tasting more delicious than that little meal we ate in the tiny office. When we were all full we agreed to adjourn to the courtyard for a postmeal promenade and business talk.

Delgaudio opened the discussion. "You seem disappointed that you've been given this wonderful chance to move to a bigger club. You must know that we have just moved up from the fourth division and that we plan to spend a great deal of money so that we can move up to the second at the end of the season."

"That's what Massesse said last year, Mr. Delgaudio."

"Perhaps so, but we have more capital than Massese. With us you will become famous. You have already made the headlines today—you're the most expensive purchase yet in third-division history. And one other thing," Delgaudio paused as if to emphasize his words, "we have bought you so that eventually we can sell you to a first-division club."

"But Massese said that last year too, Mr. Delgaudio."

The conversation went on like this for some time and might have ended without any agreement if I hadn't asked the inevitable question. "How much money are you going to give me?"

"We thought 500,000 lire [$1,000] a month might be a fair salary," replied Delgaudio.

"That's not enough," I said, trying desperately to maintain a poker face in spite of the joy welling up inside me at the prospect of doubling my salary.

"Well, I suppose we could go as high as 600,000 lire," said Delgaudio.

"What about bonuses?" I asked, quickly getting used to the idea of living in Naples.

After a brief consultation with his colleagues, Delgaudio proposed a very generous 50,000 to 100,000 lire for every point earned by the team (in Italy and everywhere else but in the United States a team gets two points for a win and one for a tie), and 100,000 lire for every goal I scored.

I agreed in general but stipulated that before I signed anything I had to speak to Massese, because I expected some money from them too.

I had less success with the hard-nosed front office at Massese. The club was overjoyed to be receiving 100 million lire and sharing it with me had not even been considered. I finally got them to promise me $15,000. Unfortunately, we never discussed when I would get the check and after I signed with Internapoli they refused to pay me. I tried everything I could think of to make them live up to their verbal agreement. I even went as far as getting my mother to return to Carrara so that she could go to the club and argue on my behalf. Finally, after my mother's tenth visit to Massese, the club officials told her not to come again since they would never give me the money because they had never promised to do so.

A few years later when Lazio and I were both doing well the Massese club had the gall to call me and ask if I would persuade Lazio to come up to Massese for an exhibition game. My answer consisted of only two words but each was worth at least $7,500 in the satisfaction I felt when I hung up.

After I was released from jail I was given four days' leave in order to collect my gear from Massese. I was in my grandmother's house in Carrara for less than eighteen hours when I received a frantic call from Internapoli asking why I hadn't come straight to Naples. The press, it appeared, had been waiting for me that morning and now both Internapoli and the press were terribly upset.

I agreed to leave the next morning and take a flight from Pisa to Rome and then another from Rome to Naples. "No, no, you must take the train from Rome so we can have someone waiting for you at the station," shouted the voice at the other end.

I asked, "How will anyone know me or even find me in that enormous station?"

The Internapoli spokesman's "Don't worry, our man will find you" wasn't any solace.

I worried all the way to Naples. I had never played in Naples (Massese played all its games in the northern section of the third division and Internapoli, in the southern section), so I was certain no one in the city would recognize me on a soccer field, let alone in a busy railroad station.

As the train reached the fringe of the city, I became extremely nervous. If I wasn't picked up at the station I had a real problem—I had forgotten to ask where the press conference would take place.

I needn't have worried. No sooner had I stumbled off the train with my two heavy cases than a rotund, middle-aged man came running up to me.

"Giorgio Chinaglia! Welcome!" He kissed me on both cheeks and took my cases.

As relieved as I was to see this jovial Neapolitan I didn't believe it was possible he had picked me out of the crowd. "But how did you know who I was?" I asked with wonder.

His bewildering reply may not have made much sense but it sent my spirits soaring: "I could see in your face that you were a great soccer star."

CHAPTER 3

LIKE MOST PROFESSIONAL CLUBS, the Cosmos give their players a day off following a game. The only ones who report in are those who didn't play and any members of the team who need treatment for injuries. On my days off I try to put in a full day's work at my office or attend a business-related activity, then spend the remaining hours with my family—my daughters, Cynthia and Stephanie, and my son, George.

Every morning before breakfast I take a walk around the garden, giving my crazy monster of a German shepherd dog, Sammy, a run, and then spend a few minutes meditating about how lucky I've been. Although I never cease to thank God for the success I have enjoyed and the comfortable life my family and I lead, in the quiet of early morning I feel it most strongly. How remarkably my life has changed since my youth in Carrara and Cardiff. As I stand and gaze at our Mediterranean-style house, pool, tennis court, and three acres of gardens, I often think of that always hungry boy and his dreams and have mentally to shake myself to convince myself the view is real.

Don't get the wrong impression. Even though I was once very poor I have no guilt complex about my acquired wealth. I'm a firm believer in capitalism. My Italian communist friends can harangue me as much as they want about the glories of a state-controlled economy and an equal division of income; my socialist friends in Britain can continue to tell me how necessary nationalization of industries is; and my young American teammates can exhort me all they want about the need for redistributing the nation's income—they're wasting their breath; I will remain a capitalist until my dying days. I am overjoyed to be living in a country in which every citizen has the chance to reach as high as his ambition drives him. Providing wealth is acquired honestly, I see no reaason why a person should not be proud of his or her achievements. I am.

I am also very enthusiastic about the Warner organization. As far as I'm concerned, their executives are the ones who put American pro soccer on the map. Without their faith in the future of soccer—translated into the millions spent in bringing Pelé and the other stars who followed to the United States—soccer would still be a minor sport here competing with lacrosse and curling for a minimum of coverage in the sports pages.

I'm a real organization man when it comes to the Cosmos. Every time I walk into the Warner lobby and glimpse the enormous blowups of the 1977 and 1978 championship teams I feel an enormous sense of pride at being associated with them.

Upstairs on the Cosmos floor that same strong feeling overwhelms me when I see the six larger-than-life photos of Pelé, Beckenbauer, Alberto, Marinho, Tueart, and me. (The photos cleverly conceal the doors of the six elevators and even now I feel a little disconcerted when I see my likeness disappear when the elevator doors open.)

As chairman of the board at Warner Communications, Steve Ross runs an international entertainment conglomerate that includes: Warner movies; Warner, Electra, Asylum, and Atlantic records; Warner Books; cable television; and many other subsidiary companies—but as far as Steve is concerned it is the Cosmos, a $25,000 investment in 1970, that is now unquestionably the pearl in the multijeweled Warner empire.

Steve is charming, firm, generous, and a hard-nosed negotiator, and, like so many powerful American businessmen I have met, he's never too busy to listen and talk to his rank-and-file employees. If I become a business entrepreneur in my later years I will use Steve as my model.

On more than one occasion Steve has sought my advice, however. One time in 1979 Steve had Pino Wilson's future on his mind when I entered his spacious but comfortable office. Pino, a dear friend and former teammate, played for the Cosmos in 1978 as a loan player and was all set to play again in 1979. One of the top defenders in Italy, an Italian international, and a player the Cosmos badly needed, Pino had arrived in New York the week before but shortly thereafter returned to Lazio.

Steve said he had heard Pino was asking for more money before he would fly back here. He asked if I had spoken to Pino recently. I admitted that Pino had called me the previous Saturday to complain about the difficult choice he had to make. Lazio was now offering him the general manager's position when he retired if he would stay with the club and not accept the Cosmos' offer. Pino thought I could persuade the Cosmos to pay him more to offset his losing this managerial opportunity. I had been upset that he expected me to intercede for him since I had already let it be known that I thought the Cosmos were overly generous in the amount they had agreed to pay him. He was now $35\frac{1}{2}$ years old, an age when a soccer player should

no longer expect to receive the type of contract the Cosmos were offering. And now Steve was asking for my
advice.

Let me quickly mention here that all those stories cir-
culating that I run the Cosmos because of my relationship
with Steve couldn't possibly be true even if I wanted them
to be for the simple reason that no one—and, believe me,
I mean no one—tells Steve what to do or changes his mind
if he has a strong opinion on a subject. The suggestion
that I run the team is absolutely ridiculous. Granted,
Steve does ask me for my thoughts on many matters deal-
ing with the game of soccer and I'm only too happy to
oblige. But that's as far as it goes and it's no different
from any other boss asking an experienced employee his
opinions. As far as our socializing is concerned we concentrate on having a good time, and rarely talk shop.

What advice to give Steve on that occasion was a bit of a
puzzle. I wanted to have Pino back with the Cosmos and
certainly he deserved to receive a fair salary for his services. The question was, What was fair? I didn't feel I could
endorse overpayment even for a friend. That was my advice to Steve. Whether he was swayed by what I said
when he discussed the matter with Nesuhi Ertegun (chairman of the board of the Cosmos), his brother Ahmet
(president), Rafael De La Sierra (executive vice president), or coach Eddie Firmani I don't know, but I do
know Pino never came back from Lazio and is now slated
to be Lazio's manager when he retires.

As I've said before, I consider America to be one of the
few places left in this world where a man of ambition
can achieve whatever he strives for. Moreover, like so
many others who acquire citizenship in an adopted country, I've become an ardent nationalist. It's absolutely corny

I know but I'm in love with America. Peppe, my manager and friend, knows this and quite often he shrewdly uses my newly found patriotism to win me over to his way of thinking.

Thanks to Peppe, I've been blessed with great success in my business dealings here in the United States, which is the exact opposite of my ventures in Italy where I lost a large fortune. My investments have done well and the companies he advised me to do promotional endorsements for have proved to be good choices: Chevrolet (I drive a '69 Corvette), Pony and Spalding (two of the finest sporting merchandisers in the country), Progresso Foods (the large East Coast food distributors), and the prestigious Fidelity Union Trust have all gone out of their way to treat me royally.

Although I have a manager and an attorney I try to do as much of any negotiations as possible myself. Once the preliminary contacts are made by Peppe I step in. I've done this since my days at Internapoli. It's not that I didn't trust my father then to look after my interests or that Peppe doesn't have the expertise today; it's just that I feel I should be responsible for my own destiny. Why should I delegate important decisions affecting my career, my investments, or my family's future just because I can afford the services of professional experts?

Then too life would be one big bore if I sat back and watched others become my mouthpiece. I enjoy handling business matters nearly as much as playing soccer and at times it's nearly as exciting.

These are the reasons why I can never understand why so many soccer players have agents to do all their negotiating. They all have tongues in their heads so why should they give an agent a hefty part of the income from their short-lived careers. Rarely does a player last more than ten years in top-flight soccer or earn enough money to throw it away. But I'm sure that was hardly on my mind when I joined Internapoli.

By the time I reached Naples' Vomero Collana Stadium, the home of Internapoli, on that hot afternoon I could hardly keep my eyes open. I had left Carrara that morning at six to make all the connections and had overindulged in a heavy lunch on the train. Concentrating on the questions during the press conference took a great deal of will power. I yawned so often I had the whole roomful of reporters rubbing their eyes and yawning in turn. I did surprisingly well answering the questions and was impressed by the large turnout. At Massese we had normally drawn five or six reporters for a press conference; that afternoon there were over twenty. The Internapoli spokesmen had been right: compared to Massese they were big time.

All the single players at Internapoli slept in the building adjoining the stadium. Each had his own large, well furnished room and after the press conference ended at four I was taken to mine. The large double bed was a welcome sight. I didn't bother to unpack; I just collapsed onto the bed.

Luckily I hadn't touched my cases, for within minutes of dozing off someone shook me violently saying, "Let's go, Chinaglia; the car's ready."

"Car? What car?" I mumbled. Still half asleep, I was pulled off the bed and guided outside to a waiting car. "Where am I going? Not another press conference, I hope?"

"Of course not, Chinaglia. You've got to join the team in the mountains for *ritiro*."

Before the car's motion lulled me back to sleep it occurred to me that every time I joined a new team in

Italy I was sent to the mountains. I was so tired I didn't bother to ask which mountains I would have the pleasure of running around, up, and over. When I woke up I did ask how it was possible for me to go away for *ritiro* when I was due back at my army camp in two days. I should have known that as usual the army's wishes were incidental whenever the more important demands of professional soccer were involved.

My guide explained that if a club needed a particular player who happened to be doing his army service all the secretary had to do was request a certain number of days' extension of any weekend pass or furlough. Thus, Internapoli's secretary was going to ask for such an extension for me and I would be staying in the mountains for at least ten days, perhaps even a month.

I quickly discovered that life at Internapoli was hectic because the staff was disorganized, so I suppose I shouldn't have been surprised when on the third day of *ritiro* the secretary of the club came rushing into my room at four in the morning to bellow, "Hey, get packed, your train leaves at six."

"Where am I going?" I asked.

"Back to the army; we forgot to ask for an extension for you. You're AWOL!"

Internapoli had some promising young players when I joined them, including Pino Wilson who was to become my close friend then and later on at Lazio.

It wasn't surprising they had a lot of potential talent because they were never shy about spending money to get what they wanted. Indeed, they had recently spent hundreds of thousands of dollars strengthening the team. Balestrieri, Girardo, Russo, and Valle had all come from the first division and the club had tried to get more experienced players, but few first-division stars were willing to drop down into the third, no matter how attractive the cash. The big money Internapoli spent proved in the end to be a smart investment since the club attracted large crowds and went on to become the richest club in third-division history. The club's enormous expenditures on their youth teams was also a financially shrewd move as many of their graduates were later sold to first-division teams. As a matter of fact, six of my teammates went on to play in the top division.

Although Internapoli had spent a vast amount of money preparing the team for third-, and possibly second-, division soccer we started off the first half of the 1967–68 season as if we meant to go down to the fourth in record time. The team lacked cohesion and our midfield seldom controlled the games as the front office expected they would.

I was having a terrible time up front. In some games I was lucky if I got two passes. By the middle of the season I had scored only one goal. I attributed that to the lack of support from my teammates, but the fans figured it was due to a decided lack of talent on my part and soon I was known sarcastically as "Mr. 100 Million Lire."

Fortunately for me the team brought in a new coach, Oscar Montes, an Argentinian. Without question he was one of the most eccentric people I've ever met. At his first meeting this funny, warmhearted, and definitely a little crazy man announced that "this team has a forgotten center forward who could score many goals but the rest of the team doesn't seem to know he exists. From now on we are going to play the ball to him."

With Montes' new system I scored nine goals in the next 10 games. We didn't lose any of the remaining 17 games and moved up to fourth place in the final standings. We began to improve at the gate too, finishing with a

15,000 average attendance—a remarkable figure for third-division soccer.

By the end of the season I had attracted the attention of some of the first-division clubs: A. C. Milan, Bologna, Inter-Milan, Florence, and Lazio. It was accepted that, barring a serious injury, the 1968–69 season would be my last in the third division. After what had transpired at Swansea it was difficult for me to believe that I was on the verge of becoming a first-division player. All I needed now was to play well in my last season at Internapoli and my childhood dreams would come true.

I played well enough in the '68–'69 season with Internapoli and escaped serious injury on the field, but I still nearly missed my big chance of moving up to the first division due to my own foolishness.

The incident occurred one night after I left the American Bar in Naples. I often went there after our Sunday games or on my day off on Monday. The doors of the Internapoli clubhouse closed at eleven-thirty at night and so as not to wake up the caretaker or his family I was in the habit of climbing up the drainpipe to my sixth-floor room. This particular night I returned from the American Bar with Paolo Pini, a reserve midfielder, and proceeded to climb the pipe while Paolo watched. When I reached the fourth floor I suddenly realized, to my horror, that the pipe was slowly coming away from the wall.

"Paolo!" I yelled hysterically. "The damn pipe is falling off!" As I spoke a shower of bricks grazed me on their way down. I gave another yell: "I'm going to be killed, Paolo!" More bricks hit the paved marketplace adjoining the club entrance. Lights turned on and people opened their windows to see what was causing all the commotion.

Still uttering cries of anguish I tried to descend the pipe. As I slid down I noticed, much to my disgust, that

Paolo had run off leaving me stranded. I was level with the second floor when the pipe finally parted from the wall. I flew onto the pavement. In shock, momentarily, I was certain I had broken every bone in my body. I heard the caretaker yell to his wife as he ran out of his apartment, "Call an ambulance."

The neighbors joined in inspecting my bruised body. "Don't move him, whatever you do," I heard one say.

"Serves the robber right," observed an elderly woman.

"He's no thief," said the caretaker, "it's Giorgio Chinaglia."

While the caretaker explained to the gathering crowd that it had been my own window I had tried to enter, I attempted to move the various parts of my aching body. Slowly, I realized that there was nothing wrong with me other than a severe case of embarrassment.

I stood up and made my apologies. The unhappy neighbors went back to their homes complaining about the behavior of young men in general and soccer players in particular. I still had to explain my actions to the caretaker.

"But, why didn't you knock on the door if you wanted to come in?" he complained.

"Well, it's one o'clock and I didn't feel it right to wake you or your family," I responded truthfully.

"Don't worry about how late it is," he said kindly, "next time you knock on my door, Giorgio." He patted me on the back affectionately.

He paused at the front door. "By the way, is anyone else coming in later?"

I remembered my friend Paolo and quickly replied, "No, I'm the only player who went out tonight."

About ten minutes later I heard the pitter-patter of stones hitting my window. Outside looking up at my room was a worried-looking Paolo. "Let me in, Giorgio," he whispered.

I opened the window and said in my most pleasant voice, "Paolo, you bastard, if you want to come in wake up the caretaker."

"But, Giorgio, I'm not on the first team; he'll kill me," he moaned.

I fell asleep gleefully listening to the caretaker shouting and swearing at the young and unfortunate Paolo.

From this scary experience with the drainpipe I learned a very good lesson: never take chances when there are ways to avoid them. The next day I set out to find a long ladder. It was surprisingly easy, for the men who were building a swimming pool on the other side of the stadium had several. From that day on, until I left Internapoli, I borrowed a ladder any night I went out and hid it in some bushes near the clubhouse entrance.

It was while I was at Internapoli that I met Connie. It was in the summer of 1968. She and her girlfriend Vivien from Chicago were walking along one of the picturesque streets in the Vemero section of Naples. I was with a few of the players from Internapoli and one of them said, "I bet you 1,000 lire that they're English." Another player said he thought they were American.

My teammates' remarks were not nearly as clever as they might seem since the girls were conversing in English. As I was the only one of our party fluent in the language, I had the pleasant task of identifying the nationality of the two dark-haired beauties.

When the girls entered the Danieli restaurant for a snack we stood outside watching them through the window. They were amused by our interest and smiled back at us. When they came out my friends pushed me ahead and told me to start chatting.

I've been shy since I was a child and it took me three

blocks before I found the nerve to say something. The girls had stopped by a magazine stand where Connie bought an American magazine. One of the players dug his knuckles into my back and gave me a shove. I stepped forward and in a near-whisper said, "You're an American, aren't you?"

Connie nodded and said she was. She then said to her friend Vivien in Italian, "I told you they would ask that!"

As soon as my teammates heard the girls speaking Italian they pushed me aside and took over the conversation. I remained on the fringe of the group the rest of the afternoon. I didn't waste the few opportunities I had of talking to Connie though; before we parted I arranged to visit her house and listen to some of her American records.

Connie's parents had been living in Naples ever since her father retired from the American army. From the very first day I visited them they made me feel like one of the family. I jumped at every chance to return to their house. After two years in the land of my birth I was finally enjoying my nonsoccer hours.

I sorely needed their warmth and kindness for at this time in my life I was in pretty bad shape. I hadn't adjusted to living in Italy. Making new friends had been difficult—and so I was lonely. Added to this, Italian social customs frequently exasperated me. I had not yet become accustomed to the action and occasional rudeness of Italian street life, where the slightest altercation brings with it a wide variety of obscene hand signals and choice obscenities and where getting onto a bus means a shoving match whenever there are more than two people waiting. I suppose it's the individualistic nature of Italians that makes them behave so rudely in public but I still wasn't happy with their attitude regarding others. In conversations I seldom heard anyone express concern about other less fortunate Italians. Everyone seemed to be looking out only for number one.

Another aspect of Italian life that bothered me was that none of the young men of my age I met had a job. Instead, they sat around the tables at sidewalk cafés sipping espresso or wine. Whenever I would ask one what he did for a living he would answer, "I'm a student."

But the Italian custom I found the most difficult to accept was having a chaperoning mother tag along on those few occasions I got up the courage to ask an Italian girl for a date. For someone who always had enjoyed the company of women, in both Cardiff and Swansea, a chaperone was quite a shock. Strangely enough, even though Connie was a fully liberated American girl I was content to share her with her parents. To be honest, I would have to admit that Connie and I did not have a typical romance at all for the first year. It was all very platonic; I spent a lot of my time telling her how much I missed my girlfriend in Swansea. We listened to her records, ate her mother's delicious cooking, and watched television. Apart from an occasional walk to go shopping, we never went out of the house. Her parents must have thought me odd. The time came, though, when I realized Connie was no longer just my buddy but someone I was beginning to love. I definitely did not want to get serious, since my whole life was devoted to getting to the top in soccer, so I began to visit Connie less often and for shorter periods. Sometimes I would arrive at her house, stay only five minutes, then make an excuse to leave. When I was with her I was so afraid of divulging my new love for her that I became tongue-tied. I knew my behavior puzzled Connie but not knowing then that she too was falling in love I didn't realize how unhappy I was making her.

Finally, I stopped visiting her house altogether. About a week later one of my teammates brought a note into my room. Connie had delivered it personally and was waiting outside for an answer. The note was brief and since it caught me unprepared, had a lot of impact.

Dear Giorgio,
    What kind of friend are you? You haven't come to see
me for eight days. Please come this evening.
                                        Connie.

I went out onto the balcony of my room, looked down
at her and saw how worried she looked. She saw me and
I waved. Her face lit up with a loving smile and I knew
then what I should have known long before: that we felt
the same way about each other.

There was no turning back after Connie's visit. Within
six months I found the courage to ask her to marry me.
She accepted my proposal and I was the happiest man
in Naples.

A week after my proposal I found out that I was going
to go to Lazio, the famous Roman club in the first division. Now I was the happiest man in the whole country.

In Italy soccer is considered more important than anything. It certainly carries greater weight than politics, re-
ligion, love, or marriage. I knew this so I suppose I
shouldn't have been so angry when the diehard soccer
fans cringed when I joyfully announced that I was going
to get married.

"Get married! Are you mad?" seemed to be the unanimous reaction.

The consensus was that I would be a fool to get married
before I was firmly established in first-division soccer.
Over and over, I was told I was going to ruin my career
as the transition from the third to the first division was
tough enough without the added responsibilities of married life. My coach at Internapoli said so, the coach at
Lazio said so, and my father, who came over from Wales
to advise me, said so. Even my future in-laws thought
Connie and I should wait.

Bowing to the pressure because I thought they meant
well, Connie and I agreed to wait for eighteen months,

but as the months went slowly by, with Connie in Naples and me in Rome, we found the separation too much to take. We made up our minds that we would get married as soon as the 1969–70 season was completed, regardless of all the advice.

Thus on July 9, 1970, we were married in the San Vincenzo Pallotta Church in Naples and left on our long-awaited honeymoon.

It was hardly the honeymoon we expected, however. I had made the mistake of discussing our honeymoon plans with one of the players on the Lazio team, a player who shall remain anonymous. A more obtuse individual never existed.

Imagine this romantic scene: in the cabin of our Sardinia-bound boat we, the newlyweds, were happily embracing. After nearly two and a half years we had at last been left alone. There was a knock on the door. More congratulatory telegrams? Or another bouquet of flowers? No, it was my new teammate and his wife clutching a bottle of champagne and four glasses. Gleefully they shouted, "Surprise! Surprise!"

The next few days were unbelievable. We were a constant foursome, no matter how hard Connie and I tried to avoid them. They sat in the hotel lobby waiting to pounce on us whenever we left our room. Invariably they greeted us with "What shall we do now, kids?"

It was like living a horrible nightmare. Connie tried to be game about the unhappy situation I had unintentionally arranged, but I knew that if I didn't find a way to break up the quartet I would not be forgiven the rest of my life. To make matters worse, my teammate and I couldn't see eye to eye on any subject and our arguments the first two nights about music and soccer lasted until the early hours of the morning.

On our third day in Sardinia I knew I couldn't take it anymore. I woke Connie up early and told her to pack our bags. We were on the boat to Naples before my team-mate and his wife got up. Unfortunately, we only escaped from one disastrous situation to another. I figured the best place to go for privacy would be a seaside resort. I was familiar with one near Rome—Fregene.

We arrived there late in the evening to discover there were no hotel vacancies anywhere. Out of desperation I called a Lazio fan who I knew lived in the town. He was only too happy to offer Connie and me a room for as long as we wished to stay.

So for the rest of our honeymoon we stayed with this friend—and his eight children, his wife, his father-in-law, his mother-in-law, and his two brothers-in-law. And in the traditional Italian style I spent most of my time with the men and Connie with the women. Only Mel Brooks could have devised a stranger honeymoon.

CHAPTER 4

DURING THE EARLY PART of the 1979 season I had been worried about the fate of Eddie Firmani. For weeks he had been having problems with the Cosmos and Warner Communications chiefs who compose the Cosmos board of directors and I sensed the dispute was coming to a head. It was clear that Eddie's days were numbered unless he quickly changed his ways and became more accommodating. Eddie and I have been friends for many years and I had urged him repeatedly to be more positive and diplomatic in his dealings with the front office. A warm, friendly guy, Eddie is also very stubborn and doesn't accept advice easily, even from his well intentioned friends. He has a tendency to think he is infallible on soccer matters. I suppose you can't blame him too much for thinking he knows it all when you consider his highly successful playing career in both England and Italy, his years of coaching the Charlton club of England, and the first-rate job he did of building up Tampa Bay into one of the great teams in the NASL.

But in spite of all his expertise, Eddie often fails to remember that soccer in the United States is completely

different from that in the rest of the professional soccer world, and that the Cosmos brand is the most different. The Cosmos, after all, are one of the few soccer
clubs in the world that are run along the lines of a big
corporation. Like the structure of giant corporations, the
various levels of command are fairly evident at the Cosmos, and any coach who wants to succeed with the club
has to realize quickly that satisfying each of the echelons
is part of the job. By this I mean the Cosmos general
manager, Krikor Yepremian; the Cosmos executive vice
president, Rafael De La Sierra; the president, Ahmet
Ertegun, as well as all the high-ranking officials in the Warner Communications executive suite. To dismiss these
people as interfering novices in soccer matters is not the
best way to stick around. A Cosmos coach has to try to
please these executives as much as he does the fans and
members of the team.

Yes, the Cosmos are run like a big business. And why
shouldn't this be so? Professional soccer is as much a business as it is a sport. Certainly as far as the owners are
concerned, soccer of the last twenty years, as it has been
presented in the top soccer countries, has been at least
70 percent an entertainment business and 30 percent pure
sport.

People like Steve Ross, Jay Emmet (President of Warners), Ahmet Ertegun, and Neshui Ertegun (chairman
of the board of the Cosmos) are not only accustomed to
success but also to getting 100 percent cooperation from
their employees. It was clear to many of us that Eddie was
not even agreeing 80 percent of the time with any of the
four top executives at Warner.

I suppose it was primarily the arrival of Marinho
(whom Eddie had not wanted) that had deepened the
rift between Eddie and the top management. Eddie called
Marinho a "glamor boy" and a luxury his team could not
afford: a player whose brilliant plays were fun to watch

but a player whose style interfered with a team game. It's true Marinho is an individual who can perform brilliantly in any position: he's a marvelous defender, good in midfield, and a dazzling forward, but no matter where he plays he is always attacking in the opponent's penalty area. Put him in at left back and he will spend half the game racing through the opponent's penalty area looking for goals. Play him at midfield and he will take more shots at goal than any of his forwards.

Marinho is one of those players every club owner wants but there are few coaches who can handle him. Personally, I never believed Eddie really knew what to do with him and consequently never used him right. I'm still not sure if that was intentional or because Eddie didn't understand Marinho's zesty fun-loving approach to life, but I do know Eddie thought Marinho too individualistic to fit into his overall team planning.

Another reason for Eddie's annoyance with the Cosmos board of directors was their insistence on having three big exhibition matches during the 1979 season. The proposed matches with Coventry City of England, the full Argentinian national squad, and Bayern Munich of West Germany had the Cosmos fans drooling, but as far as Eddie was concerned it was simply a case of bad planning, for they would place an unnecessary burden on the players and the coaching staff. The fact that the big revenues from the gate would help to pay for some of the expensive Cosmos purchases had little impact on Eddie's thinking.

Eddie did a marvelous job with the Cosmos. He organized a loosely connected group of individuals with a jumble of various styles and personalities into a formidable championship team and no one can take the credit away from him.

One coach of whom I have very fond memories, a coach quite a bit different from Eddie, is Juan Carlos Lorenzo,

one of the world's top coaches. Now coach of the famous
Boca Juniors, a team he had led to two South American
Championship titles in 1977 and 1978 and a runner-up
medal in 1979, Lorenzo was one of the key figures in the
growth of my soccer career. A genuine soccer expert, he
helped me bridge the tremendous gulf that existed between third- and first-division soccer when I arrived at Lazio in the summer of 1969.

I was lucky to have him as my mentor in that first year.
His wealth of experience included starring in the center
forward position with Boca Juniors, and Sampooria and
Genoa in Italy and Rayo Vallecano of Spain; coaching
the 1962 and 1966 Argentinian World Cup teams; gaining promotion for Lazio in 1964 in his first season with
the club; then a spell coaching Rome; and then back with
Lazio for the 1969–70 season.

As a former center forward there was a lot he was able
to teach and I took advantage of every opportunity to
listen to all his skillful coaching. He was very kind to me
despite his reputation of being a tough guy who produced
rough uncompromising teams. And his teams *were* rough.
In 1965 he was banned from coaching for three months
for running onto the field during a Lazio–Turin game to
urge his team to get physical and "kick some legs." During
the 1966 World Cup his team was called "a bunch of
animals" by English coach Alf Ramsey after a fierce match
between Argentina and England at Wembley Stadium.
Later on when coaching Atletico Madrid in the early
1970s, he was in hot water with the top European clubs
for his hard-nosed and ruthless approach to the game.

Unfortunately for Lorenzo, he didn't have much to
work with when he came back to Lazio in 1969. Apart
from Pino Wilson, Giuseppe Massa, a very talented
winger, and Ferruccio Mazzola (the younger brother of
the famous Sandro of Inter), the players available to
Lorenzo could not be classed as championship material,

at least not in the strong Italian first division. With the club heavily in debt, there was little hope that Lorenzo would be given the wherewithal to buy top players to reinforce the team. Lazio, after all, had experienced a difficult decade, going down to the second division a number of times. It had gained promotion to the first division in 1964, finished in 14th place in both '65 and '66, gone down again in 1967, and happily had won the second-division championship in 1969, a few weeks before my arrival.

But despite the successful season in the second division, the Lazio team knew that life would be a series of challenges when it came up against the big boys of the first division. The 1968–70 period saw some of the best soccer in Italy's history so we were about to face superteams and superstars, the likes of which had not been seen in Italy since the great days of the 1930s when Italy won the World Cup twice in its two attempts.

There was A. C. Milan with the flawless Roberto Rosato and the West German star Karl-Heinz Schnellinger on defense; Giovanni Lodetti, a superb midfield general; and the "golden boy" of Italian soccer, Gianni Rivera, doing amazing things with the ball on its forward line. The other Milanese team, Inter, still had many of its stars who had taken Europe by storm in the mid-sixties when it won two European Cup finals and barely lost a third. Among them were the Italian national team captain, Giacinto Facchetti, one of the best backs of modern soccer; Tarcisio Burgnich, an equally fine defender; Mario Corso, a brilliant midfielder or winger; and the elegant world-class forward Sandro Mazzola. Up in Turin, backed by the wealthy Fiat company, Juventus also could field a team of stars. Lining up for Juventus were the fabulous Dino Zoff, one.of the top goalkeepers in Europe since World War II; sweeper Sandro Salvadore, the ironman of Italian soccer; Helmut Haller, the veteran West German midfield star; Fabio Capello, the stylish forward; and Piet Anastasi, the young striker whose purchase a year earlier had cost a world record $1 million.

Other powerful teams were Florence, Turin, and Cagliari, the surprising club from Sardinia which had built a tremendous team around Luigi Riva, the exciting goalscoring superstar in this exciting era of Italian soccer.

The national team was enjoying its best period since the 1930s. It had won the European Nations Cup in 1968 and even though it was easily beaten in the final of the 1970 World Cup by Brazil (when it broke down against the marvelous Brazilian offense of Pelé and company) it was a world-class team in every respect. Alas, it has not been able to recapture that wonderful balance and teamwork since.

At first I was not fearful about facing all the remarkable talent in the first division: I was too thrilled at being a part of this exclusive club to worry about the reputations of our opposing players or teams. Moreover, I was engaged to be married, I was young, healthy, and getting paid quite a bit of money each year to play my favorite game. And I felt I could score against anyone.

The bubble soon burst. Within a short period I discovered that eagerness and confidence were just two of the many things necessary for success in this extraordinary first division. The game was so much faster than anything I had been exposed to in the third division and the technique of the players was far better than I had yet come across in my seven years of pro soccer. For example, the most difficult maneuvers were being performed effortlessly. In addition, I found it difficult to anticipate what my more experienced teammates were trying to do with the ball, so many of their passes to me didn't connect. I was very worried about my shortcomings.

Lorenzo, however, refused to let me worry. He explained that he had expected I would find the transition from the third to the first division difficult. His solution was simple—together we would work on improving my skills: sharpening my shooting at goal, increasing acceleration from a standing position, learning how to escape a marking opponent in the penalty area, shielding the ball more effectively with my body when pressured by the strong and sometimes suicidal tackling of Italian defenders, and endlessly improving my chest traps so that I could turn quickly even when receiving chest-high balls. Gradually I got my confidence back.

Much to everyone's surprise, we started off the 1969–70 season as if we meant to take the championship or *scudetto,* as it is called in Italy. Lorenzo initiated me into the rigors of top soccer by bringing me in as a substitute in the second game of the season against Bologna. I didn't score but I was pleased with my performance. Lorenzo apparently also thought I did well for he started me in the third game—a game at home in Rome's Olympic Stadium, a white marble oval masterpiece with a capacity of 90,000. Our opponent was the mighty A. C. Milan, the 1968 champion and easy winner of its first two games of the new season. The famed Milanese defense, with Roberto Rosato, Angelo Anquiletti, and Karl-Heinz Schnellinger outstanding, cut off all avenues to its goal. Every time I received the ball two or three defenders converged on me. Flying legs, chopping elbows, crushing tackles, and violent body blows! What had I gotten myself into? I hadn't taken such a pounding since I played rugby.

But far more upsetting than the physical hammering I was taking was the ease with which the Milanese defenders seemed to anticipate what I was going to do with the ball even before I knew. I left the field at halftime wondering once more if I would ever adjust to this class of soccer.

In the dressing room Lorenzo took me to the side away from the other players. I figured I was in for a tongue-lashing. Instead he said, "Just keep playing the way you are, Giorgio. In a few months you'll be scoring goals with regularity." He patted me on the back and walked away.

There are numerous examples of knowing coaches uttering a few well chosen words at halftime that have produced startling changes in both the teams and their players. Lorenzo's words had that effect on me. I went out on the field feeling that a great weight had been lifted from my shoulders. With confidence I held onto the ball and even ran at the defense with it. Twice I evaded Schnellinger with quick acceleration only to shoot wide.

And then it happened. Pino Wilson hit a long ball out along the right side of the penalty area. The Milan defenders seemed to think it was going out of play and that I couldn't reach it before it went over the goal line. But by the corner flag I controlled it, then, dribbling past Anquiletti, I cut in toward goal. As Fabio Cudicini came out of his goal I curved it around him. I was already throwing my fists up into the air in celebration before the ball slammed into the back of the net. It was one of the greatest single moments of my life, and I didn't stop running around the field until my teammates grabbed me by the halfway line.

As I stood there in the middle of the field, waving to the delighted 80,000 fans and listening to the roar of their approval, I knew I had been accepted by the Lazio supporters. And in Italy having the fans on your side is probably more important than having the support of the coach or manager. On the other hand, if the fans don't like you, they can unnerve even the strongest-willed player with their tremendous booing and catcalling, and the inevitable flying bottles, cushions, and cans.

It was the only goal of the game so we beat one of the very best teams in Europe, the team that would win the World Club Championship the following week when it defeated Estudiantes of Argentina. A photograph of me scoring the goal hangs above the desk in my study: it is one of my most prized possessions.

Another red-letter day for me occurred two weeks later when we hosted the defending champion, Florence, at the Olympic Stadium. I scored two goals in our magnificent 5-1 victory. Scoring two goals in one game in the Italian first division is considered a remarkable feat and right away the news media mentioned me as a possible candidate for the Italian national team.

By the end of October we were fourth in the standings after nine games. But our fine pace in those opening games couldn't last: we just didn't have the quality players needed or a strong enough bench. Within a few weeks we were near the bottom of the standings struggling in every game, even having difficulty holding opposing teams to tie games at home. It certainly seemed that another drop to the second division was in store for us. I found it nearly impossible to score goals and often wondered in those dark days of winter if I wasn't more to blame than anyone else for our distressing situation.

In retrospect, the biggest difficulty I was having at that time was trying not to let opposing defenders infuriate me to the point that I would lose my concentration. In the ferocious world of Italian pro soccer defenders know all the nasty ways to distract you. Since all pro defenses are based upon tight man-to-man marking, the defenders have many opportunities to provoke their opponents, not only when the ball is within playing distance but also when the ball and the referee are at the other end of the field. So many times I was kicked in the ankle or shin or elbowed in the face while fifty yards away from the action only to receive a profuse apology for "accidentally" running into me that it's a wonder I didn't retaliate.

I often smile when American reporters ask me to name the dirty defenders in the NASL. In my opinion players in the NASL are all gentlemen compared to the tough hatchet men of Italy. Even the more physical stoppers of the NASL like Steve Pecher of Dallas, Peter Simpson of New England, Willie McVie of Toronto, and John Craven of Vancouver are Mr. Nice Guys in comparison. Steve and the others can send their opponents sprawling with a fierce body check or bloodcurdling tackle, but the Italians are past masters of the hidden foul that the referee doesn't see. In addition to the physical abuse the Italian defenders hand out they are artists at such infuriating infractions as shirt-pulling and holding.

In the spring of 1970 we recaptured our earlier form. All of a sudden we were playing marvelous soccer and enjoying some brilliant wins. We beat Palermo, 4–0, then had two dazzling triumphs, winning 3–1 over second-place Inter and defeating third-place Juventus, 2–0. We completed our schedule with a 4–1 rout of Bari and a 0–0 tie at Brescia. The point earned at Brescia moved us up to ninth place. Our spring showing augured well for the next season. If we could play as well as we had for the last two months we knew we would be contenders for the championship. Many of us on the team thought we could emulate Cagliari, the unfashionable club from Sardinia, which had won the season's championship with only a few top players.

I had managed to score 12 goals in regular season play, a respectable total even for a veteran in the defensive-minded world of Italian soccer. The leading scorer in the league was Riva, that masterful center forward, who had 21 goals to his credit and was the main reason Cagliari had taken the title.

My 12 goals apparently caught the eye of the national team coach Ferruccio Valcareggi, for I was included in the list of the 40 players the Italian Federation picked for the 1970 World Cup. Although I was not included in the final list of 22 players that was sent to FIFA, the mere fact that a rookie like me was even considered did much for my confidence that spring and inspired me to work harder.

I had many reasons to be a happy and contented 22-year-old at the conclusion of the 1969–70 season: I married Connie and moved into a beautiful apartment on Via Baldo Degli Ubaldi, a street in a pleasant and picturesque area of Rome near St. Peters; A. C. Milan was trying to persuade Lazio to sell me; and I was rich enough to invest heavily in real estate. All in all, life was nearly perfect. As for the 1970–71 season, I couldn't wait for it to begin.

Well, the season finally came but it was a complete disaster for Lazio. In our first home game in September we lost to Cagliari, 4–2, and set the dismal pattern for the coming months. It seemed we were swamped by just about every club in the league, both at home and away.

It was a particulariy bad period for me. In my first season for Lazio the press and the fans had been comparing me to the great Silvio Piola, probably the greatest center forward in Italy's and even Europe's history. Silvio, who was also tall and well built, had played for Lazio from 1934 until 1943, when the club, thinking he was over the hill, let him go at the age of 30 to Turin. Much to the embarrassment of Lazio, Silvio continued to score goals in the first division until 1954, by which time he was 41. Many Roman papers had carried headlines in 1970 demanding that Lazio not make another center forward mistake and allow me to go to one of the various clubs who were bidding for my contract. In 1971 the same journalists who had earlier been pushing me for the national team were now blaming my poor performances on my marriage and filling their columns with near-slanderous stories about Connie and me. The fans became just as unfriendly. My departure at this time would probably have drawn a tumultuous cheer from both groups.

Connie and I found our lives in Rome becoming un-
bearable. On several occasions some Lazio fans drove
around our apartment block honking their horns and
shouting obscenities about me. Everywhere we went we
ran into people ready to criticize or taunt us. It was common practice for strangers to rush up to Connie in the
marketplace and insult or ridicule her until she would
leave sobbing. It was hard to reconcile the adulation of
the Lazio fans a year earlier with their terrible behavior
of that period. (Later on, when Connie was expecting
our first baby, she was so unnerved and unhappy because
of the Lazio fans that I finally had to send her back to
Naples to stay with her parents. This, of course, made life
even more difficult for me. Missing her as I did I became
miserable and short-tempered.)

I was forever getting into arguments or fights with anyone who taunted me or Connie. An evening out for cock-
tails and dinner often ended with an unpleasant scene.
Dancing had always been a problem for Connie and I
since other couples would surround us in a tight circle
and stare and grin at us so that we would feel uncom-
fortable. Some people were determined to make it even
worse. On one occasion at the Number One Club in Rome,
two Frenchmen continually asked Connie to dance even
though they could see how unhappy I was with their
cutting in. Finally one of them took off his glasses, smiled,
then stood there challenging me to do something about it.
In those days it didn't take much to send my blood rushing to my head. I reacted quickly, knocking both him
and his friend to the floor with just two punches.

A similar incident occurred a few months later at another nightclub. Connie was heading back toward our
table after a trip to the powder room when she was stopped
by a young man who had his leg on a chair across the
aisle. I was no more than a few tables away so I saw
Connie pointing to his leg and asking him to remove it.

He did move his leg but then put his arm across the chair and turned his back toward her. Connie tapped him on the shoulder but he ignored her. By this time I had gotten my hackles up so that when he moved his arm only to replace it with his leg again I was really fuming. I picked up the nearest ashtray and threw it at him. Then, pushing my way through the tables that separated us, I lifted him off this chair and threw him down onto the floor. I was about to punch him when Connie pleaded with me to leave him alone. Friends and acquaintances in the club came over to calm me down. The young man, they said, was a well known troublemaker and I would be silly to let him upset me so. As angry as I was I managed to control my temper, but only after insisting he leave the club.

Although I was in numerous fights in those days I never started any; I was always provoked. Unfortunately, it didn't take much to provoke me. It wasn't until I came under Tommaso's influence in my mid-twenties that I was mature enough to face ugly situations without losing my self-control. "As long as you believe you are right, who cares what others say?" was Tommaso's favorite remark whenever I repeated a particularly nasty criticism to him. As a matter of fact, by the end of my stay with Lazio I was the one who usually broke up fights. However, I never shook off my early reputation as a fighter. Tales about the pugilistic activities of "Chinaglia the Bully," continued to be favorite fillers for Italian newspapers when hard news was scarce. The fact that I had dropped out of the "fight game" made no difference; reams of copy were devoted to Chinaglia's "battered victims."

A typical example of the press' disregard for the facts was their covering of the altercation that followed our 1–0 loss to Milan in 1971. I had missed a couple of easy chances in front of the Milan goal and knew some people would be upset with me; nevertheless, I was not prepared for the discussion which followed in the clubhouse. Some of the directors yelled that I was to blame for our team's defeat that day as well as our current bad streak. And why was I to blame? Because I had gotten married.

"You are more interested in lovemaking than Lazio," one of them screamed across the crowded clubhouse lounge at me. Once again I was ready to fight but my friend Vona, the club secretary, held me back. He pulled and I pushed and as we grappled I leaned against the huge glass partition in the center of the lounge. Suddenly there was a tremendous bang as the glass shattered. The sight of the once beautiful broken plate glass ankle deep on the carpeted floor only enraged the directors more. Vona hurriedly pushed me through the debris out of the lounge. This time I didn't resist even though the near-hysterical executives were still yelling at me.

The press had a field day with the glass partition episode. Reports of my "violent conduct" made most of the headlines the following morning. Most papers reported that I had engaged in fights with a varying number of directors and players and all of them had me breaking the partition on purpose, either with my fists, or, as one imaginative Milanese scribe stated, "with a vicious butt of his head."

Unfortunately, the U.S. news media has tried to keep the "Chinaglia the Bully" image alive. In 1979 I was portrayed as the one who started the Giants Stadium brawl between some of the Cosmos players and the ground crew. I was also the one who got the blame for initiating the fights that occurred during the Cosmos–Vancouver game in 1979.

As far as the unpleasantness with the ground crew was concerned, I was trying to be the mediator. In previous practices some members of the cleanup crew had made a regular habit of jeering and yelling abuse at us, and it seemed clear to me that if they kept it up there was going to be a serious confrontation. On that July day the nasty comments from the ground crew were beginning to affect our nerves, since unlike the match situations, where players expect a noisy crowd reaction, at practice sessions the only criticism we expect or want to hear is from the coaching staff.

After one particularly filthy comment from the stands I finally went up there and told one of the workers to cut it out. He pushed me and I fell backward over two rows of seats. When I got up half of the Cosmos team were around me scuffling with the workers. Some of the players and the workers were hurt but thankfully none seriously. Unfortunately, the matter didn't end there for me because the workers brought a civil suit against me and I received the usual adverse publicity—all to the effect that Chinaglia was the bad boy of American soccer (note that the press in America was just as eager to typecast me in the villain's role as the Italian press had been).

My reputation as the bête noire of American soccer was clinched after the July 15 game against Vancouver at Giants Stadium. Once again I was the center of controversy despite trying to play peacemaker. It was a rough game but the fighting didn't start until the 72nd minute when Eskandarian tackled Willie Johnston, Vancouver's Scottish international winger. They both fell to the ground and started to hit each other. Fearing for Eskandarian's face, which had only recently healed from surgery, I immediately ran over. As I reached them Vancouver's Phil Parkes grabbed me in a bear hug and while he was holding me John Craven punched me in the face. By this time all the players had arrived, either to separate the fighters or to join in. When peace was restored referee Keith Styles gave red cards to Eskandarian, Johnston, Craven, and me.

But that wasn't the end of the evening's fireworks. Trevor Whymark yelled an obscenity at me just as I passed the goal on the way to the tunnel. By now, furious at being ejected by Styles (who I maintain made the worst decision any referee had made in the NASL in 1979), I was in no mood to take any more harassment. My response was to run after Whymark. As I did, others joined in the chase. First Pelé ran out onto the field from the touchline; he was in turn chased by his bodyguard, Pedro Garay, as always seeking to protect him. Then, of all people, Peppe Pinton, sweet and gentle as he is, came racing onto the field. Whymark and I had in the meantime been surrounded by the players and many fans, who had eluded the security guards. Our whole group appeared to be swinging at anything that moved. The melee went on for ten minutes before the security guards were able to restore some semblance of order.

For me it was a disastrous afternoon: I had been ejected from the game (this had happened only once before in my career); I had a bruised face; and my faith in the NASL referees took another nosedive. Styles had been making obvious one-sided calls before the fighting even started. I wasn't the only one who thought the referee had let the game get out of hand even though he called a total of 48 fouls before the game was finally over. Even now, in retrospect, it seems inconceivable that I was punished for trying to restore order. But what was much more distressing to me was the fact that my undeserved reputation as a troublemaker was reinforced by an eager press.

In direct contrast to the previous year our team did not improve in the second half of the 1970–71 season. We suffered a terrible winter in Italy with enormous snowfalls followed by weeks of mud. The bad weather affected us more than most teams since our players preferred hard grounds, particularly some of the smaller members of our team like Ferruccio Mazzola and Giuseppe Massa.

We won only five games out of 30, finishing second to last with only 22 points. In the Italian first division the bottom three clubs are relegated to the second division so we were destined to go down along with Catania, the bottom club with 21 points, and Foggia, the third from the bottom with 25 points.

There is little doubt that the 1970–71 season was the low point in my soccer career. I scored only 7 goals in regular league play; we were relegated to the second division; and worst of all, Lorenzo, the man I continued to admire, the man who took such a special interest in me, was fired. His dismissal was, of course, due to his inability to keep us in the first division, yet for some inexplicable reason Lazio replaced him with another coach who had suffered the same fate—Tommaso Maestrelli of Foggia.

There was one redeeming feature about that season, however, for I managed to get my first experience in a European cup tournament. Lazio was selected by the Italian Federation to play in the Fairs Cup (now called the UEFA Cup). In the first round we were pitted against one of the great names of international soccer, Arsenal of England, which was the defending champion. We tied 2–2 in Rome (I got both goals in a rough and at times ugly match), but lost in London, 2–0, and thus were eliminated.

In the evening of that extremely physical game in Rome there was a shocking incident at the Augusta Restaurant when many of the Arsenal and Lazio players fought each other in a free-for-all slugfest. This time I watched in shocked silence along with one of the players on the Arsenal team, an old friend from my Swansea days, John Roberts, the fine Welsh international center back. Since we had played together as teenagers, we had a lot to talk about as we sat early in the evening watching the teams exchanging presents and souvenirs as is the custom when foreign teams meet. Both of us had come a long way since our apprentice days sweeping the stands at Swansea, and we were reminiscing and telling ourselves how lucky we were compared to many of our former teammates who were now either out of soccer entirely or struggling in one of the many semipro leagues in the British Isles. All of a sudden our pugnacious defender, Giuseppe Pappadopulo, grabbed the ear of Bob McNab, Arsenal's international fullback, and before anyone with sense could intervene at least half of the players went outside into the alley to fight it out. There was a tremendous commotion both inside and outside the restaurant as perplexed officials and the harried restaurant staff tried to restore order.

John and I drank our drinks like two proper gentlemen and considered the whole affair kind of juvenile. Even though we realized that the fighting was a result of the brutal tackling and the anger of the afternoon, neither of us felt sympathy for any player reliving events that occurred five hours before. One of the fundamental reasons for pro soccer players' shaking hands at the end of matches is to forgive and forget all that took place on the field. Yet here were ten to twelve first-division players engaged in one of the worst fracases in the history of professional soccer and ruining a pleasant banquet.

It was a night I and many others from Lazio and the Arsenal camps never wanted to see repeated. And while on the subject of experiences I'd like to avoid repeating, I hope I never have another season like that long, depressing one in 1970–71.

CHAPTER 5

I DEFINITELY HAD a negative attitude the day I was introduced to Tommaso Maestrelli in the Lazio clubhouse lounge in the summer of 1970, in spite of his impressive appearance: a magnificent physique, a handsome face, and a thick head of hair sprinkled with streaks of gray. What, I said to myself, could have prompted Lazio's owner, Umberto Lenzini, to hire him? If Lenzini did not blame Tommaso for Foggia's poor season then why should he blame Lorenzo for ours, especially since he had refused to let Lorenzo spend money on new and better players. I wanted Lorenzo to be given another chance.

Tommaso stepped over to me and in a gentle voice said, "So we are on the same team now, Giorgio. I hope you will help me get Lazio back to the first."

I nodded and mumbled a few noncommittal words then backed away, but within a week I couldn't deny that Tommaso was one of the grandest persons I had ever met. One reason for his appeal was his age. He was in his late forties and therefore old enough to be more of a father figure than the usual drill sergeant type of coach. We soon all loved and respected him. His cure for problem players may have had a great deal to do with our acceptance of him. His solution was simple: a quiet evening at home with his family. Maestrelli's talking out the problem while eating a deliciously cooked meal worked wonders. By the time dessert was passed around any difficulties the player had or thought he had were solved.

Tommaso and I became good friends very early in that 1971 summer. For a while I had been considering being transferred away from Lazio but when he heard this he came to my apartment and said, "You must stay with us, Giorgio. I need you. And I promise you, Giorgio, we will have a great team."

I agreed to stay and never regretted my decision.

A few weeks after he came to Lazio we played the Swiss team Winterthur in the Alps Cup (open to selected Swiss, French, and Italian clubs). I had tonsillitis with a high fever and told the interim coach, Flamini, I was sick. (Another ridiculous Italian soccer league rule is that a new coach cannot go into the team's dressing room until the new season starts.)

"What's wrong, Giorgio?" the coach asked.

"I have a temperature of 101 and my doctor says I have tonsillitis," I replied.

"You'd better go home then," he said, and off I went.

Outside the dressing room Maestrelli was talking to Umberto Lenzini. When he spied me he came over and asked, "Where are you going, Giorgio?"

"I'm going home; I'm sick."

"No, you're not," he exclaimed quickly in his quiet but spellbinding voice. He guided me to a quiet spot near the dressing room before continuing. "Look, Giorgio, you must do this for me. We've got to put a stop to the team's losing streak. I need you out there, Giorgio, because you are the key to this team's success. I knew when I was coaching Foggia that you were the difference between a struggling Lazio and a winning Lazio."

"But I can hardly stand up," I pleaded.

"Don't worry," he said. "Stay right here and I'll get a lemon."

He came back bearing the treasured fruit, the juice of which he made me gargle right there with some of the puzzled ground crew watching.

"That will get the pus out. Now if you can't run just walk around. You'll see, you will score today."

I scored a hat trick in the first half before being taken out so I could go home to bed. After that game I never hesitated to follow any advice Tommaso gave.

Against Perugia in that same year I was injured in the first half and forced to have eight stitches in my leg. Tommaso wouldn't put in a substitute, knowing that I would come out and play for him with only one leg if necessary. But I assumed that once he saw the stitches he would send in someone else. At halftime he came into the dressing room, looked at my leg as I lay on the trainer's table, and said, "Giorgio, I want you to come back. I must have you on that field. You can score against this team."

I remember shaking my head as if to indicate that someone in that room was crazy, either Tommaso for suggesting my return or me for agreeing to it, but nevertheless I got up and went back into the game. And as was always the case with Tommaso's hunches, I scored—twice, even though the novacaine made most of my left leg feel like it belonged to someone else.

It wasn't insensitivity or ruthlessness on Tommaso's part when he demanded every ounce of our strength, but a clear knowledge of just how much tolerance for pain we had. I believe he knew more about our limits than we did.

From the very beginning he managed to get us to run more than any other team in the second division. Being in great shape was necessary in the tactical system he was developing. Critics later on called it "total soccer." Tom-

maso's system was a natural extension of the idea called
the "Whirl," an attacking formation proposed in the mid-
fifties by Dr. Willy Meisl, the Austrian journalist. Meisl
envisaged all players constantly interchanging duties
and positions so that the distinction between defenders,
midfielders, and attackers would be reduced.

Tommaso, of course, was not the only coach thinking
along these lines. In Holland and West Germany total
soccer was also being evolved from the old 4–3–3 and
4–4–2 systems. He was, however, the only coach in Italy
courageous enough to test his attacking theories in a
country where soccer was totally defense oriented.

While we were competing in the 1971 Alps Cup Connie
gave birth to Cynthia. Although we had a game against
Lugano that night Tommaso sent me off to Naples in a
fast car. As usual, he knew what he was doing. I was so
overcome with joy at seeing Connie and my little daugh-
ter that I came back that night feeling like a twelve-foot
giant. I put two into the back of the net and came close
on two other occasions.

We went on to win the Alps Cup by beating Basel,
3–1, in the final. I scored two of our goals in our one-
sided victory over the Swiss first-division club. Tommaso
had been with us only three weeks yet his magical influence was already working. We had won our first-ever Alps
Cup; I had scored 10 goals in five games (three more than
I had scored in all the previous season); and we looked
like a championship team.

There was no doubt that Tommaso was a coaching
genius. I never met a man who knew more about soccer,
but more important he was an astute student of psychology. He was able to understand the psychological makeup
of each of his players and to act accordingly with each of
them so as to bring out his strengths and combat his weaknesses. Because of Tommaso, I believe that soccer coaching among professionals in modern soccer should be more

concerned with psychology and conditioning than with skills and tactics. That's why I'm so pleased that we have a man like Professor Mazzei running things at the Cosmos. Mazzei may not be the greatest tactical coach in soccer or even in the NASL, but he certainly is one of the best men around when it comes to preparing his players both physically and mentally for a game.

The strange thing about Tommaso's success with Lazio was that the club directors hadn't expected it—they wanted to get rid of him after his first few games. They didn't understand his easy, relaxed way of handling the players, nor were they happy about his offensive-style tactics. Even later, when he had been accepted by the club directors, the players, and the fans, few people thought he would get us back into the first division. I can honestly say I was the only one on the club at the beginning of the 1971–72 season who had complete faith in him and in his promise that we would gain promotion within a year.

By this time I was his great admirer. I listened as attentively to anything he had to say as the disciple sitting at the feet of an all-knowing guru does. How lucky I was to have been befriended by this giant of a man!

Tommaso took us back to the first division, as he said he would, at our first attempt. Although we didn't win the second-division championship we finished a strong second to Ternana. I scored 21 goals that season and was once more befriended by the fickle press and fans.

Tommaso was eager to let his secret weapon explode onto the Italian first-division scene. He had finally finished perfecting it. In his system everyone attacked except our goalkeeper and our two central defenders. In other words, our two outside defenders moved upfield with the midfielders every time we attacked so that we had five players supporting our three strikers. Conversely, when we defended everyone moved back to help except me. I positioned myself about 40 yards from our opponent's goal and it was from this point that many of our attacking movements began. Once I received the ball coming out of defense I would hit square (lateral) balls to our flanks, enabling our midfielders and outside defenders to catch up with the play and join in on the buildup. Italian teams used to *catenaccio*'s offense, based upon fast counterattacks with one or two strikers, were bound to be frightened by our attacking in waves in the 1972–73 season.

However, before Tommaso could utilize his idea to the fullest, he knew he had to go out and get the right players for his new system. Understandably, there were loud cries of outrage from Lazio fans (and players, too) when it was announced that the ever popular Giussepe Massa, our brilliant winger, was being sold to Inter. Tommaso explained that for the price of Massa he could buy not one but three players—and what players they turned out to be! —Luciano Re Cecconi, a marvelous midfielder from Tommaso's old club, Foggia; Mario Frustalupi, one of the top wingers in the league who had not been doing very well with Inter; and Felice Pulici from Novara, a goalie unbeatable in his day. All three were destined to be great successes in what was to be the best four-year period in Lazio's eighty-year history. In addition, Tommaso bought two other outstanding players cheaply: Sergio Petrelli, a strong defender from our archrival Rome (the club that shares the use of the Olympic Stadium with Lazio), and Lorenzo Garlaschelli, another wonderful midfielder in his Lazio days. One other star destined to play an important part in Lazio's success was defender Luigi Martini, who came from Livorno during our promotion season.

Tommaso's judgment was sound for this time, when Lazio played in the first division, it was the big boys who worried about playing us. We scared them all: Milan,

Inter, Florence, Cagliari, even Juventus, the defending champion. All of them feared a match with Lazio in the Olympic Stadium. How could it be otherwise when waiting for them were the noisest soccer fans in the world and a confident Lazio team with its unusual tactical system?

We began the season with a good game against Inter, tying 0–0 but nearly scoring on three different occasions. In our second game we beat Fiorentina, 1–0, and followed up this fine performance with a 1–1 tie with the defending champion, Juventus. Then we won the next four games, by which time we were right on top of the first-division table. Our pace slackened, however, during the winter months and Milan moved past us to take the lead, but right up to the last two weeks of the season there were only one or two points separating Milan, Juventus, and Lazio.

Despite our fine soccer displays and our strong challenge for the title we still had our share of arguments at Lazio. A few were violent, some were foolish, and most were over inconsequential matters. One such minor incident (at least it appears that way now) that nearly changed the whole course of Lazio's history occurred when Lenzini, the Lazio owner, caught Tommaso's twin boys playing soccer with a tennis ball outside our locker room on the afternoon of the Lazio–Rome Derby. He had the guards escort the two 11-year-olds out of the club area into the stadium.

Now Tommaso probably loved those twins more than anything else in the world so it was not surprising that he lost his composure when, emerging from our locker room, he discovered they were gone. He asked the players if they knew where the twins were. We didn't and we were also not too happy about their disappearance because we had adopted them as our club's mascots since we believed they brought us luck.

When Tommaso learned that Lenzini had sent them away, he left us to look for them. During the game he found them. He also found Lenzini and angrily accused him of stupidity for letting his youngsters roam around the packed stadium alone. Lenzini, equally furious upon hearing that Maestrelli had deserted his players, demanded to know why Maestrelli wasn't with them.

"Because my children come first," Tommaso countered, to which Lenzini answered, "Good, they need you more than Lazio does."

Naturally the whole of the Italian sporting media interpreted these strong words to mean that Tommaso was through at Lazio, especially since he had yet to sign a contract for the 1973–74 season. The truth was, however, that within a matter of hours both Lenzini and Tommaso had calmed down and life went on in its usual stormy way at Lazio until the next confrontation. Though I must admit if we hadn't enjoyed a 2–0 win over our archrivals that Sunday afternoon, the Lenzini–Tommaso argument might have had some serious consequences for all concerned.

The Rome game had been our fourth win in a row. This winning streak continued for another five games. Our ninth consecutive victory was against Milan. We won, 2–1, before a record paying crowd (nearly $400,000) at the Olympic Stadium and thought we had clinched the championship. (I scored both goals, one of them on a 30-yard shot that broke two fingers of Belli, the Milan goalie.)

Unfortunately, we could only earn one point in a 1–1 tie at Turin so by the last Sunday of the season Milan was one point ahead of us with 44 points, while we were tied with Juventus for second place.

We traveled to Naples where we had a tough defensive game. At halftime we received the unbelievable news that Milan was losing heavily to Verona and that Juventus was losing at home to Rome. To the excited players in our dressing room, it seemed that all we had to do was score a goal in the second half and the championship would be ours (the first time in Lazio's history).

But six minutes from the end of the game Naples scored and we lost the game, 1–0. Not that the result mattered, since Juventus scored two goals in the second half to beat Rome, 2–1, and finished up with 45 points. Milan, which lost 5–3 to Verona, was second with 44 points and we had 43.

We might not have won the *scudetto* but none of the big, wealthy northern teams were going to take us lightly again. And just to show that Lazio expected to do as well the following season Tommaso did not buy any new stars. Even the Lazio players were pleasantly surprised, because usually the top Italian teams race helter-skelter into the player market during the off-season, particularly teams expecting to challenge the titleholder. Tommaso told us that we were already a complete team and that there was no reason to tamper with its parts. He was right, of course. The strength of our fine season's performance rested upon our well developed and unselfish teamwork with everyone willing to run without the ball in support of the teammate with it. If anything, we expected to be a faster team in 1973–74.

The success of Tommaso's Lazio team was instrumental in my selection for the Italian national team. Actually, I was still a second-division player when picked for my first game against Bulgaria in June 1972. Ferruccio Valcareggi was criticized quite a bit by the northern media for picking a second-division player when there were so many fine strikers playing in the first (I was the first ever to be chosen from the second). The Milanese papers were particularly furious that Pietro Anastasi of Juventus was not chosen. Unfortunately for the rest of my national team career, these papers were always pro-Anastasi while the Roman papers supported me in what I considered to be a silly media-made feud.

Personally, I thought I was more effective than Pietro. He was faster than me, but I was stronger and scored more goals than he did. Nevertheless, playing for the glamorous Juventus team and being the world's costliest player were two obvious points in Pietro's favor. In any case, the Milan and Turin media are never impressed with the rest of the country's teams or players. After all, the four clubs from Milan (Inter and A. C. Milan) and Turin (Juventus and Turin) have dominated Italian soccer since the end of World War II, winning 22 championships out of the 27 played.

In the Bulgarian game in Sofia I came in as a substitute in the second half. It was a dream-like debut for within 30 seconds I ran onto a fine pass from Fabio Capello and drove a hard shot toward the left corner of the goal. Goranov, the Bulgarian goalie, got a hand to it, but I raced in and hit the rebound into the other corner.

As soon as I saw it was a goal, I raced over to the section where Tommaso was sitting and dedicated the goal to him by gesturing with my outstretched arms. I believe he was as excited as I was.

I was in the Italian lineup for the team's next game against Yugoslavia in Turin in September. I scored again, this time from a beautiful pass from Gianni Rivera. In the second half I was substituted and Anastasi came in. He scored too in the 3–1 win, enabling the northern press to ask why he wasn't in the starting lineup in the first place. (Incidentally, Bogie played for Yugoslavia that night.)

The next match Italy played was a World Cup qualifier against tiny Luxembourg. The game attracted the many thousands of Italians who were working in Luxembourg and when I scored Italy's first goal in the third minute they stood up and cheered for a good three to four minutes. I have always considered that goal the most important I have ever scored, even though it was against a weak team. Why? Well, I suppose it was because I knew the Italians there were waiting for a goal, a goal that would enable them to feel they had struck back at the fates that had taken them away from their homeland. To the people in Luxembourg the Italians' tremendous reaction to that goal was nothing more than noisy nationalism, but as a former emigrant I understood how they felt.

We went on to win the game, 4–0; Luigi Riva scored two goals and Capello got the fourth. Two weeks later when we played Switzerland, our opponent in another World Cup qualifier, I didn't score. This match, my fourth consecutive game, ended in a dismal 0–0 tie with both teams playing poorly. I did put the ball in the net and the referee had signaled for a goal but after the Swiss players protested he consulted the linesman and the goal was disallowed because of an offside call.

In none of those four games did Italy look as strong as it was. Many of the sporting journalists gave the team a hard time, some even writing that Italy didn't deserve to play in the 1974 World Cup finals since the only reason we were going to qualify was because of poor competition in our qualifying group. You had to admit there was some truth to what they said. Turkey, Luxembourg, and Switzerland were definitely not first-rate soccer countries.

I was chosen for the next World Cup qualifier, against Turkey in Naples. We were terrible. Our team was disorganized and never seemed to come to grips with the rough and acrobatic style of the Turks. Our midfielders weren't too good, but still our forwards were unlucky not to score at least six goals. But even if we had played another 90 minutes we probably wouldn't have scored against Sabri, Turkey's red-hot goalie. Naturally, the papers had a field day tearing apart the team and Ferruccio Valcareggi so it was not surprising, bearing in mind the powerful influence of the Italian journalists, that there were many changes in Italy's team for the next game. Only four of the first game's starting lineup were chosen to travel to Ankara for the second game against Turkey: Dino Zoff in goal, defender Tarcisio Burgnich, midfielder Franco Causio, and striker Luigi Riva. I was out and, yes, Pietro Anastasi was in.

I wasn't chosen for the Luxembourg game either, a game Italy won, 5–0, with Riva scoring four goals. But I did get the opportunity to play the second half against the fine Brazilian squad when it came to Rome in preparation for the following year's World Cup.

Ever since I first played for Italy there was one thought at the back of my mind: I wanted to play against England when the mother country of soccer came to Rome on June 12. I think not being chosen for that game was one of my biggest disappointments. I sat in the stands and watched Anastasi and Capello score in Italy's workmanlike 2–0 win, the first time in over forty years of trying that Italy had beaten England.

Italy was scheduled to go to London for a return engagement with England in November of the same year, and I promised myself that I would play so well when the new season started that Valcareggi would have no choice but to take me to England. Just the thought of stepping onto the hallowed turf of Wembley Stadium sent goose bumps up and down my spine in spite of the heat of that sweltering Italian summer.

There was another important moment for me during the 1972–73 season. Lazio drew Manchester United in the summer Anglo-Italian Cup. Before the game at the Olympic Stadium I had the honor of presenting a plaque and a pennant to my boyhood hero Bobby Charlton, the captain of Manchester. Never, even in my wildest dreams as a kid in Cardiff, did I ever think I would be on the same soccer field as Bobby, let alone share equal billing. And yet here was the man who had first played for United when I was eight and for England when I was 11 shaking my hand and calling me Giorgio. Bobby was my hero because he was the best winger I had ever seen and probably the nicest guy ever to play soccer. He was a gentleman in every sense of the word and well known for his kindness, decency, and honesty. What made the occasion even more memorable for me was the fact that within two weeks Bobby was going to retire from soccer after a twenty-year career.

The game itself was an anticlimax after the excitement of the pregame ceremonies. In a scoreless tie both teams seemed more interested in breaking legs than in playing soccer. The referee that day was Gordon Hill, who is now involved with the Tampa Bay youth development program. He spent most of his time blowing his whistle, writing names down in his little black book, and breaking up fights. He probably still hasn't forgiven me for running after a Manchester defender who had really butchered me. Gordon pushed me away from the defender and in doing so broke his hand.

The Anglo–Italian Cup was inevitably a minor disaster, bringing about bad blood between the two groups instead of the friendly feelings for which it had been designed. The traditional violence can be directly traced to the different attitudes the Italians and English players held regarding body contact. Whereas the Italians considered shirt-pulling, holding, and elbowing a normal part of body contact, the English did not. On the other hand, the Italians were appalled by how strongly the English tackled and by how much they used to shoulder charge.

Perhaps if the cup were staged today it would be more

successful, seeing how top pro soccer has become much more uniform in the last few years. But I wouldn't count on it. As far back as the 1934 "Battle of Highbury" when England beat Italy, the World Cup champion, 3–2, blood and fury have been the order of the day whenever the English and Italians get together for a soccer game.

CHAPTER 6

IN THE SUMMER OF 1973 Lazio toured the United States. As a reward for our fine season's play the married players were permitted to take along their wives, which proved to be a wise decision on the part of Lenzini and Tommaso. We all had a wonderful time and more important the strong team feeling Tommaso had developed among the players became even stronger. No one takes soccer more seriously than I, and yet I believe the best thing that ever happened to Lazio was its deliberate attempt to combine business with pleasure on that trip. If more clubs would permit families to go along on summer tours there would be fewer player defections. Certainly no one on the 1972–75 Lazio squads wanted to leave, not even when we had our periodic blowups.

By the end of the tour we were like one big family, despite having most of our luggage stolen in a Chicago hotel, losing to Pelé, Carlos Alberto, and the rest of the magnificent Santos team, 4–2, in Chicago, and having a game abandoned in· Jersey City when the crowd invaded the field. (I was about to take a penalty kick when the referee stopped the game. "The hell with the ref," I shouted at the opposing goalie, "don't you dare leave until I take my kick." The goalie, who thought I was a little crazy, shrugged his shoulders and watched me kick the ball past him. I know what he thought, but there was no way I was going to pass up a golden opportunity to score just because a few thousand people were on the field. Even though the goal didn't count, I loved watching the ball go into the net. It's the best way a game can end for a striker.)

While in America I had the opportunity to look around. I liked what I saw. Connie and I had a marvelous time wherever we went. What I enjoyed most was the luxury of walking around without being recognized by the general public. While I was having the time of my life touring the vast beautiful country, eating at some of the finest restaurants to be found anywhere in the world, and meeting the friendly outgoing Americans, Connie was realizing just how much she missed the United States. She asked me to consider returning permanently. At first I figured her wanting to live in the United States was some passing fancy that would quickly fade once we returned to Rome. But I was soon to discover that her desire to go home was very real. In fact, it intensified so much that eventually it changed the whole course of my life.

Upon our return from America we prepared ourselves for what we hoped would be a successful challenge to mighty Juventus. Going for its third successive title, Juventus hoped to be the first Italian team to win a hat trick of championships since the Turin team did it during its great four-year run of 1946–49. Turin's marvelous team was lost, incidentally, when its plane crashed into a hill near Turin. All seventeen players on board were killed, including nine members of the Italian national team. Italian soccer never quite recovered from that air disaster and its defensive mentality can be traced directly to that crash and the loss of so many outstanding players.

Juventus was a prime example of the defensive strength of Italian soccer and now for the beginning of the 1973–74 season it had purchased another top defender, Claudio Gentile, to strengthen what was already one of the best teams in the world. Its normal lineup read like a *Who's Who* of Italian soccer: Dino Zoff, probably the world's best goalie in the mid-seventies; in front of him four Italian internationals, veteran Sandro Salvadore, Gianpiero Marchetti, Luciano Spinosi, and newcomer Gentile; three superb players patrolled its midfield, Franco Causio, Fabio Capello, and Antonello Cuccureddu; and up front a trio of top-class strikers, Roberto Bettega, Pietro Anastasi, and the veteran Brazilian star Jose Altafini. At the opening of the season everyone but Cuccureddu was an international, and he too would soon be on the national team.

At first glance Lazio's customary lineup may have looked ordinary compared to that of Juventus but during the 1973–74 season we played like supermen: we had great ball control, we ran nonstop, and we communicated with each other almost perfectly. All this gave Lazio a balance and quality that hasn't been seen in Italy since.

In goal was Felice Pulici, an almost perfect goalkeeper who only had one weakness—he didn't like to move off his line to intercept high crosses.

Our four defenders, Sergio Petrelli, Giancarlo Oddi, Pino Wilson, and Luigi Martini, were nearly impossible to get by during that thrilling season. Oddi, in particular, played well above himself and looked all set to join Wilson and Martini on the national team but unfortunately he was never able to play that well again.

In midfield we had Franco Nanni, a marvelous attacking player. He and Lorenzo Garlaschelli scored many important goals as they swept up the field with the forwards. Luciano Re Cecconi, on the other hand, was the one who made goals with his marvelous passes. A complete player, Luciano was probably the star of our team and it

was a great tragedy when he was killed in 1977 during
a prank. With most of his face covered by a handkerchief,
Luciano entered a friend's store and announced it was a
holdup. He was shot and killed by his friend who kept
a gun in the store.

In attack, Mario Frustalupi was both a brilliant winger
and an imaginative midfielder. He and Luciano combined
often to set up devastating attacking moves. I was in the
middle and on my left was Vincenzo D'Amico, a highly
gifted youngster with remarkable speed and a cannon-
like shot.

And you can't forget Tommaso; we considered him the
twelfth man on the team.

In our opening game on October 7 at Vicenza we won,
3–0. The following week we beat Sampordia, 1–0, and on
October 28 we tore into the champion Juventus team
and for the first time in three years beat the famous
Turin club by a score of 3–1. Three out of three was
certainly the way to begin the season, but in the next
four weeks we were held to a tie by Fiorentina, Cesena,
Inter, and Cagliari.

Tommaso and all of us knew that we had to get back on
the winning road if we expected to stay close to Juventus,
and on December 9 we were determined to take the maxi-
mum two points when we faced Rome in the local Derby.
The word "Derby," like many soccer terms, originated
in England. It refers to any game between two teams from
the same city or town, and usually it brings out enormous
partisanship on the fans' part and overly rough play on
the players'. Some of the more famous Derbys include
Rangers and Celtic in Glasgow, Liverpool and Everton in
Liverpool, Boca Juniors and River Plate in Buenos Aires,
Turin and Juventus in Turin, and of course Real Madrid
and Atletico in Madrid. But the Lazio–Rome match can
outdo any other Derby in hysteria and violence. It was a
game that none of us at Lazio looked forward to playing.

Age nine, in my hometown of Carrara, Italy.

As part of my pregame ritual when I was playing in Italy I always greeted my fans in the "Chinaglia Corner" of Rome's Olympic Stadium.

There's one down and three to go as I make my way through a typical packed Italian defense. The 4–1 odds are nothing unusual for a striker in Italy's first division. DUFOTO

Playing for Italy against Switzerland, I'm doing what I love to do most on a soccer field—striking for goal. OLYMPIA

Scoring against mighty Juventus was always a thrill. Here I connected with a flying half-volley that left supergoalie Dino Zoff helpless.

I use my size and weight here to screen the ball from two determined defenders.

Though I don't score many goals this way, heading can be a very effective tool.

I score on a penalty kick against Roma.

Here I'm receiving a trophy for scoring the most goals in the 1973–74 season while Pino Wilson holds a replica of the club's trophy.

My coach and great friend Tommaso Maestrelli (in the sports jacket) and some of my Lazio teammates outside our practice field. From left to right: Luciano Re Cecconi, Felice Pulici, Tommaso and Luigi Martini.

This Italian magazine picture of me posing by the Coliseum had a flattering caption that read: "The two top Roman attractions."

Now that's what I call a great voice! I'm listening to a playback of "Football Crazy," my best-selling record in Italy in the early seventies.

In 1977 I shoot the ball past my old friend and former team-mate Felice Pulici as I score for the Cosmos against Lazio at the Olympic Stadium in Rome—my first return visit since I joined the Cosmos.　AP

How the Cosmos have changed! Out of the eleven players shown here before the 1977 Lazio game, only I am still with the club. Next to me in the back row are Vito Dimitrijevic, Mike Dillon, Charlie Aitken, Bobby Smith and Erol Yasin. In the front row, from left to right: Jadranko Topic, Terry Garbett, Keith Eddy, Tony Field, and Ramon Mifflin.　RICCARDO BOLDEZZI

The ball sits comfortably in the net and I jump for joy. Do I love to score!   SANTO STUDIO

The new immigrant: I fill out an alien address report card as a U.S. Immigration and Naturalization Service official looks on. I became a citizen on August 25, 1978.

JOHN McDERMOTT

Pelé—not only the greatest player ever but probably the most affectionate in soccer history.

A recent photo of the Chinaglia family. From left to right: George, Stephanie, Cynthia, and my wife, Connie.

With the chef's compliments. Former Cosmos general manager Clive Toye and I might have had our differences, but we both share a passion for gourmet food.

Here we are in China. In the last four years the Cosmos have done more than their fair share of supporting the international travel industry.

A soccer player in New York can get to know the most interesting people. Clockwise from top left, I am with tennis star Bjorn Borg; Henry Kissinger; Mick Jagger from the Rolling Stones; and opera great Luciano Pavarotti.   JERRY LIEBMAN

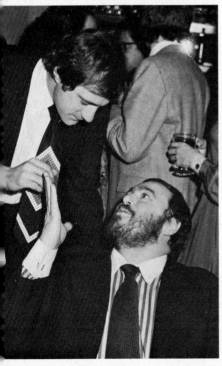

The overhead kick is probably the most exciting kick of all, especially when the ball finds its way into the back of the net. Unfortunately this ball went over the crossbar in a game against Detroit.   *NEWSDAY*

I can't stress enough the importance of running without the ball. In this game against Washington, after having passed the ball, I'm running into an open space for a return pass.   JERRY LIEBMAN

When heading, hit the ball with your forehead and keep the neck taut, but, above all, remember it is the player who can jump the highest who usually gets the ball.
JERRY LIEBMAN

Giants Stadium, July 15, 1979. Angry at being ejected (for only the second time in my career) and a little bloodied, I race back onto the field after being taunted by a Vancouver White-cap player.   JERRY LIEBMAN

I guess even referees make mistakes.   HARRISON FUNK

New Jersey Governor Brendan Byrne signs the proclamation for Giorgio's Day.

The great Johan arrives. From left to right: Werner Roth, Wim Rijsbergen, Professor Julio Mazzei, Johan Neeskens, myself, and Ray Klivecka posing the day Johan signed with the Cosmos.   JERRY LIEBMAN

I have a soft spot for this photo taken at my soccer camp. The attentive youngster reminds me so much of myself at his age. I've never forgotten the help older players gave me, and like this boy I tried to absorb everything I heard.
EILEEN MILLER

My friend Peppe Pinton and I are never happier than when at our summer camp. Coaching kids is very rewarding and also great fun.
EILEEN MILLER

Nevertheless, we had ourselves to blame for the flood of emotions that surrounded the twice-a-year meeting. For weeks before a Lazio–Rome match we would give out statements to the press and TV saying how we would murder Rome. Then with only two or three days to go we would start suggesting that certain players weren't good enough to be on the same field as us. Of course, the Rome players did the same thing, claiming that we had no players of the caliber of their Angelo Domenghini or Pierino Prati.

Sometimes the fans were so worked up before our Derby that the game could not start until some of the Lazio and Rome players went out onto the field and calmed them down. Pino Wilson and I did this chore; usually raising our arms up and down would do the trick. Of course, Pino and I also knew how to infuriate the Rome fans when we felt like it. All we had to do to get them to go berserk was to run over to their side of the stadium and stand there. And if we waved our fists up in the air and smiled all hell would break loose. But the worst of all possible insults to the Rome fans was the sight of me running toward them after I had scored against their team. If all this seems only slightly more civilized than ancient Rome's gladiatorial contests it's most likely because it is. There's a lot of the primitive left in Roman "sporting" events still. If you doubt it go see a Lazio–Rome Derby for yourself. You'll find it's all too true that Italian soccer fans frequently lose all perspective when it comes to their passionate love affair with soccer. A win by their team on a Sunday can mean celebrations all week long; a loss can mean going on a rampage against rival fans—and even players. I lost count of how many times the Lazio bus was attacked after one of our wins on the road. Smashed windows, slashed tires, and attacking mobs were commonplace. Luckily, so were the club-twirling riot police to the rescue. At home too we often had trouble with

fans, especially if we lost. And yet despite all the madness
and violence in Italian soccer the only time I was ever
personally attacked was in Varese, and of all people it
was a priest who went for me. I was just getting onto
the bus following our 1–0 win when this elderly priest
rushed at me. Giancarlo Oddi grabbed his arm as he
swung at me but the wild-eyed priest did manage to spit
on my face and unload a couple of surprising obscenities
before the police pulled him away.

The Lazio–Rome game in December 1973 was a tense
and exciting game with the roar of the crowd threatening
to destroy our eardrums. It was 1–1 until the 68th minute
when I scored with what was in all modesty a terrific shot.
We won the game, 2–1, and I'm sure there are still Rome
fans who would like to kill me now for my little demonstration in front of them after I scored.

Just as we had hoped, our win over Rome sent us into
high gear for the rest of the season. We won the next
seven out of eight games, including another big Derby
victory over our archrival, 1–0. So it was no wonder that
life for Lazio players and fans was blissful during late '73
and early '74. We took over the leadership from Juventus
around Christmas and stayed there for the rest of the
season. Among some of our notable victories was another
3–1 win over Juventus in Milan in February. This time I
scored two goals and was now leading the goalscorers in
the first division with 11 goals.

We beat Ternana, 4–2, and expected to clinch the
championship against Turin in our next game on May 5
but we lost, 2–1. There was now a chance that Juventus
could still take its third consecutive title if we lost to
Foggia the following week. That following Sunday, May
12, we met Tommaso's former club Foggia in front of
90,000 at the giant Olympic Stadium. Hundreds of extra
police were on duty when we ran out of the tunnel. They
had been called out to protect us from our own fans com-

ing onto the field if we won. As it happened, the Lazio fans (notorious for their unruly behavior) were surprisingly cooperative that afternoon. Perhaps the dull defensive game had a lot to do with it. Foggia, which was desperately trying to avoid going back to the second division again, was out to earn a point even if it meant stationing eight men back in their penalty area.

With 10 minutes left to play the score was still 0–0, and it wasn't because we weren't trying. We attacked the Foggia goal time and time again but to no avail. Then we lost Luigi Martini who broke his shoulder. The sight of Luigi walking off affected all of the Lazio players; it was like a bad omen because Luigi had played in all of the season's games. But just as we were ready to give up trying to get through the packed Foggia defense, one of our players was fouled in the penalty area. We were awarded a penalty kick.

As the penalty kick taker for Lazio I had taken many important penalty kicks (every penalty is vital in Italy where most games are won by a single goal), but here was a championship waiting for us if I could only make one solitary successful kick.

Talk about pressure! The roar of the 90,000 spectators peaked just as I made my run toward the ball. I tried to stay calm as I looked up at the Foggia goalie. He knew that if he didn't stop the ball it might mean second-division soccer; for me it might mean the most coveted honor in Italian soccer. I approached the ball as if I were aiming for the left side then hit it hard and low into the right corner. The goalie dived to the left and the ball shook the back of the net. I had scored! I thought of many things all at once: We had broken through the near-impenetrable Foggia defense. We were going to be champions today after all. How sad the goalie looked as he dived. Thank God I didn't miss. That goal was for Tommaso. I would run to embrace him.

But I couldn't get to Tommaso. Hugged and pum-
meled by my teammates I couldn't move. The referee
finally ordered us back into our half of the field for the
kickoff. It was then that I raced across to the touchline to
hug and kiss the master coach.

In the remaining few minutes Foggia tried to attack,
but we had given up only five goals all season and we
weren't going to allow lowly Foggia to add any. The game
ended with a thunderous roar from the crowd. After we
shook hands with the sad Foggia players, now doomed
to the second division, we ran around the outside of the
field in the traditional lap of honor. Then, both crying
and laughing, we hoisted Tommaso onto our shoulders
and were overjoyed to hear the roar of approval increase
for our beloved coach.

We stayed on the field for 15 minutes and the cheering
never stopped. All of us in the stadium—the fans, the
players, the coaching and managerial staffs, even the ticket
sellers—celebrated what we had achieved together. Compared to that dark day in May 1970 when we went down
to the second division, this day when we became number
one in the whole of Italy became even more glorious. If
I had my way, there would be a law that every soccer
player would have the chance to be a part of at least one
championship team. I think all of them deserve at least
one moment of complete glory.

That championship season was doubly memorable for
me because I had been picked to play against England in
London in November. Since I was a youngster in Cardiff
I had dreamed of one day playing at England's Wembley
Stadium—a stadium used only for cup finals and inter-
nationals since its construction in 1923. Playing against
England at Wembley is probably the highest honor a
soccer player can attain other than winning a World Cup
championship medal. This still holds true even though
England (the home of world soccer ever since the birth

of organized soccer there in 1863) is no longer the supreme power of international soccer that it was for sixty years. However, England is still tough at home, for foreign teams visiting Wembley seldom win—only six so far out of 66 games played there.

Apart from the symbolic importance of playing at Wembley, there was an additional reason why this game was so special for me. It gave me a chance to prove how wrong those English and Welsh clubs were to let me go to Italy in 1966 when they had the chance to get me cheap.

It may have been a typical gloomy English November day to the 75,000 people in the stands at Wembley when I followed our captain, Giacinto Facchetti, onto the halowed, lush Wembley turf, but to me, burning with an inner fire, it was as warm as summer.

The big athletic English team lined up alongside us for the national anthems: Peter Shilton in goal; Paul Madeley, Roy McFarland, Bobby Moore, and Emlyn Hughes on defense; Tony Currie, Colin Bell, and Martin Peters in midfield; and Mike Channon, Peter Osgood, and Alan Clarke on attack. (Kevin Hector, now with Vancouver, came on later as a sub for Clarke.) Our team lined up as follows: Dino Zoff, Luciano Spinosi, Mario Bellugi, Tarcisio Burgnich, Giacinto Facchetti, Franco Causio, Romeo Benetti, Fabio Capello, Gianni Rivera, myself, and Luigi Riva.

The match itself was not the type the English spectators had come to see. It was a hard-fought defensive battle with stacked defenses and fast-breaking counterattacks. Oh yes, the English team under Sir Alf Ramsey was just as defense oriented as the Azzuri (our national team's nickname) with its 4–4–2 formation. Gianni Rivera was our best player and certainly the star of the game. He did things with the ball that had the English players gasping in awe. Yet as brilliant as Rivera was, we rarely got through the tight defensive wall set up by England's

Madeley, McFarland, Moore, and Hughes. It wasn't until the 88th minute that we were able to score the game's only goal. I moved down the left side of the penalty area and took a hard shot. Peter Shilton in goal couldn't hold onto it and Fabio Capello ran in to hit the loose ball past him.

We had beaten England at Wembley and the former Swansea Town reject had helped do it! The next day I went to Cardiff to spend some time with my sister Rita. While I was there a newspaper reporter called from Swansea to ask if he could see me that day. I told him I had to take the three-thirty train back to London but that he could interview me over the phone. I can still remember his opening question, mainly because the same thought had occurred to me many times.

"In retrospect, Mr. Chinaglia, would you say having to leave Swansea Town was a blessing in disguise?"

CHAPTER 7

THE DAY AFTER GIORGIO'S DAY in 1979 I took the Maestrelli family and my Roman friend Sergio Valente on a tour of New York City. We finished off the delightful day of sightseeing with a visit to Studio 54. While there a photographer from one of the Italian news agencies took some pictures of Connie and me dancing. Sergio laughingly suggested that I had better not buy *Oggi* or *Gente* or any other of the popular Italian magazines the following week since the caption to the photo would probably read "Chinaglia's Mysterious New Love."

I laughed, but not too heartily, since I knew only too well how much truth there was in Sergio's jest. Italian magazine writers stoop to any depths to get a story and they are experts at distorting simple and innocuous incidents. On more than one occasion when Connie and I were photographed in Roman nightclubs, her face was deleted and another woman's face superimposed so that I could be accused of having an affair with another woman. Even more frequently the photographers purposely took obscure photos of Connie and me and identified her as

"Giorgio's Most Recent Discovery" or "Chinaglia's Newest Flame."

In 1974 a pornographic magazine had a picture of a nude taking a shower with a caption that read, "The shapely twin of Connie Chinaglia loves to keep clean." The woman in the picture, the magazine claimed, was the exact double of Connie and the accompanying article described a day in Connie's life. Another typical trick of the gossip-monger branch of the Italian press was the frameup. I ran into this gutter-style journalistic trick when I left a nightclub in the summer of 1973. I said goodnight to my two companions, Pino Wilson and Giancarlo Oddi, and went to my car. As I got in, a female voice in the backseat said, "Hello, Giorgio." Before I had finished my "Who the hell are you?" a whole battery of flashbulbs began popping around my car. The next day I had a lot of explaining to do when Connie opened up the centerfold of her newspaper and saw two pages filled with photographs of the car, the girl and an astonished Giorgio Chinaglia.

Because of this incident and others like it, I spent more time talking to my lawyers discussing libel suits than playing soccer. And it wasn't only the magazines. There are more than fifteen newspapers in Rome alone and these all try to fill their pages with what they consider to be newsworthy gossip, scandals, and sex.

I never got along with writers from the scandal sheets. Unlike many other well known Italians, I refused to be cowed by their powerful influence and their ability to ruin a person's reputation. Instead I let them know just what I thought about their interfering, snooping, and deceit. Sometimes I was lucky, and they printed a small apology in fine print in an unlikely place.

Even now the Italian press seems to enjoy distorting news about me. When Sergio returned to Rome follow-

ing his few days in New York with me he mentioned to a
magazine writer that I was writing this book. Sergio gave
the information in good faith in the belief it might help
me and the book. If he had asked me first I could have
told him what the result would have been. The ensuing
article was a vicious attack on me filled with outrageous
sarcasm in which I was compared with Liz Taylor (a ridiculous parallel was drawn between her many husbands
and my many alleged lovers) and described as the biggest
boozer in international soccer and one who spends a fortune each year on clothes. Sergio was so upset when he saw
the article he immediately sued the magazine. Eventually,
the magazine rewrote the article for his approval but the
damage had already been done.

One of my favorite places in Rome was Jackie O's, a
sleek and plush disco on the Via Bon Compagni. I had
my own table there which was always reserved in case I
made an appearance. Connie and I went there frequently,
as did many of our friends. It probably was the in-spot
of Rome during the mid-seventies. In 1975 after Connie
had moved to our new home in New Jersey and I had
started to commute back and forth for over a year, my
visits to Jackie O's were by necessity made with members
of the Lazio team or other male friends. So guess what
the papers and magazines had to say about this? "Giorgio
Chinaglia and Wife to Be Divorced"; "Giorgio Gives Up
on Women"; and what must have seemed to some editor
the logical conclusion to all this—"Giorgio Chinaglia, the
Homosexual Soccer Star."

Anyway, on that May night in 1979 at Studio 54, a
gentleman dressed in a white dinner jacket was dancing.
Around his neck he wore a plastic board which periodi-
cally (apparently when the music excited him to an ex-
treme degree) lit up with about 1,000 tiny red light
bulbs. Despite his wild get-up there was something regal

about his manner which reminded me of Prince Giovanelli, who entertained my friend Sergio and me one
night at Jackie O's when we were trapped inside by a mob
of Lazio fans waiting for our exit.

I mentioned this to Sergio and we both began reminiscing about that night—the night we and the rest of Rome
celebrated Lazio's one and only championship victory in
its eighty-year history.

Along with Sergio and the members of the victorious
Lazio team, I had driven around Rome in the Lazio bus in
the middle of a slow procession through the thousands of
celebrating Romans and we finished our journey at Jackie
O's. We assumed we were safe from the marauding masses
of Lazio soccer fans who were tying up traffic throughout
the downtown area of Rome with their celebration. But
someone in Jackie O's must have squealed, for by ten
o'clock there were three or four thousand happy fans trying to break down the door to get at us. It was a friendly
and festive crowd, but I had seen such crowds turn into
frenzied mobs before and I had no intention of going
outside to face them. My teammates and the others in
the club felt the same way so no one ventured out. The
longer we remained inside, the bigger the crowd outside
grew. By four in the morning everyone in Jackie O's was
tired of dancing and worried about getting home. This is
where Prince Giovanelli came to the rescue with his one-
man show. For over an hour he stood in the middle of the
dance floor and had all of us in stitches with his impersona-
tions, monologues, and renditions of some of the famous
passages from Italian literature. We didn't leave Jackie
O's until five-fifteen that morning when, thanks to the
police, the street outside was finally cleared.

That night and the following week there were a host of
Lazio parties. Not only had we won the title but we had
done it decisively, winning 18 games and losing only five.
I headed the goalscoring list with 24 goals so it was a

double triumph for me. It was also a double victory for Tommaso as he won the Coach of the Year award.

What a glorious season we had had! From the very beginning Tommaso had convinced us that no team in Italy could stop us from achieving what up to then had been the impossible: a championship for poor old Lazio, a club which until Tommaso's arrival had rarely enjoyed much glory among the giants of the first division.

I only wished we could have had Tommaso's driving force guiding the Italian national team that summer during the World Cup fiasco. He would never have permitted the Italian team to have been split by dissension, nor would he have allowed personal considerations to affect his choice of players. Ferruccio Valcareggi, on the other hand, had obviously been too loyal to his older players. Few of the young promising players were given the chance to prove themselves in Germany in 1974. Many of the younger reserve players on the team were unhappy, and the conflict between youth and veterans came out into the open. There was also the usual friction between the northern and southern players on the team. Adding fuel to the fire were we three Lazio players (Pino Wilson, Luciano Re Cecconi, and me) who were upset at not having more of our fellow teammates on the national squad. We had a fair gripe. Usually when a team wins the championship the same year as a World Cup, at least six of its players are chosen for the national team. We felt that not choosing players like Giancarlo Oddi, Felice Pulici, Lorenzo Garlaschelli, and Mario Frustalupi was just another example of northern prejudice against non-Milanese or non-Turin players. What made it even more frustrating was that these Lazio players would have given the team the fire and the spirit it obviously needed.

After our feeble display against Haiti, Valcareggi made only one change for our next game against Argentina— Anastasi came in for me. I watched the game from a seat in the stands since I was "being punished" for my controversial behavior during and after the game with Haiti. Neither team played well and, like all soccer players watching others play, I was in agony seeing all the mistakes and believing I could do better. The Argentinian game, the second game in our group series, had to be won if we expected to move into the final round of the World Cup. We knew Poland, the fourth team in our group, was one of the best teams in the tournament and if we failed to beat Argentina (which had lost to Poland in its first game) we would have to tie or beat the Poles, which we didn't really expect to do unless we improved considerably.

One of the few players who impressed me that day was Rene Houseman, who also played for Argentina against the Cosmos at Giants Stadium in 1979. He gave his markers, Fabio Capello and Romeo Benetti, a terrible time with his marvelous dribbling and running. He also scored a fine goal in the 15th minute of the game, hitting a beautiful chip from Carlos Babington into the net with a tremendous shot. Ten minutes later he nearly scored another.

Italy managed to tie the score when an Argentinian defender, Roberto Perfumo, put a Benetti shot into his own goal but we never looked as if we were about to score again. Our midfield was disorganized; Rivera was having a terrible game and Capello spent so much time chasing Houseman he was ineffective. As for our strikers, Riva and Anastasi were hardly in the game and neither was willing to run for loose balls. Causio came in for Rivera in the 66th minute without any noticeable improvement in the midfield. The game ended in a 1–1 tie. We knew we weren't playing up to our potential but we would have one more chance when we faced Poland in Stuttgart.

On June 23, 1974, we lined up against Poland with the

following team: Dino Zoff, Luciano Spinosi, Francesco Morini, Tarcisio Burgnich, Giacinto Facchetti, Sandro Mazzola, Romeo Benetti, Fabio Capello, Franco Causio, myself, and Pietro Anastasi.

Poland's team was: Jan Tomaszewski, Anton Szymanowski, Wladyslaw Smuda, Jerzy Gorgon, Adam Musial, Sygmunt Maszczyk, Kazimierz Deyna, Henryk Kasperczak, Grzegorz Lato, Andrzej Szarmach, and Robert Gadocha.

Our game started at four in the afternoon, as did the Argentina–Haiti game. If we could tie with the Poles it didn't matter how many goals the Argentinians scored against Haiti, but if we lost then Argentina could move into the next round by scoring at least two more goals than Haiti.

At halftime Argentina was winning, 2–0, and we were losing by the same score. It was all Poland in the first half. The speed and brilliant teamwork of the Poles had us defending almost the whole 45 minutes. It wasn't surprising when they scored two goals just before halftime. The first came from a leaping header by Andrzej Szarmach and a few minutes later the elegant midfielder Kazimierz Deyna smashed a cross from Anton Szymanowski into a low corner of the net. Anastasi and I up front weren't getting much help from our midfielders and both of us were discouraged as we left the field.

A minute after halftime I was taken out and Roberto Boninsegna came in. This time I was careful not to make any gestures even though I felt Valcareggi was wrong to replace me. Our team did get into the game more in the second half and we managed to pull one goal back when Fabio Capello scored with a beautiful low shot. For the last 15 minutes we attacked often, but the speedy Polish midfielders and defenders never gave our forwards room to shoot carefully and the final whistle blew with Poland still leading, 2–1. We then heard that Argentina had won,

4–1, which meant the South Americans finished with a better goal difference than we did, 7 for and 5 against to our 5 for and 4 against.

It was a sad ending for all of us. We hadn't played well, and I probably played as badly as anyone. Italy had expected Luigi Riva and me to score lots of goals; neither of us had scored any.

After all the time I had spent dreaming about being a part of a World Cup it was particularly depressing to admit I hadn't enjoyed one minute of it. Even the pre-Cup preparation had started out badly. For two weeks before the tournament we had been stuck in a hotel outside Stuttgart under prison-like conditions. We hadn't been allowed out of the grounds even in the evenings after training sessions. There had been German police with machine guns and police dogs everywhere; the security was very tight because the West German government sought to forestall any repeat of the 1972 Olympics massacre when 11 Israeli athletes had been murdered by Palestinian terrorists. We hadn't been allowed any contact with the outside world, other than with members of the press.

I hadn't eased the pretournament tension any by my attempts to make some sense out of the Italian team's tactics. One of the big problems of Italian national teams in the late sixties and seventies was what to do with Gianni Rivera and Sandro Mazzola. Both played the same type of game—attacking midfield general—and although world-class players, they never played well together. I thought that to have both on the team was a luxury we couldn't afford as we generally relied on a strong defense and speedy counterattacks.

Many of the players agreed with me so I decided to talk to Valcareggi about it. Accustomed as I was to having the freedom to discuss such matters at Lazio with Tommaso, I was surprised at the vehemence of Valcareggi's reception (though choosing to visit him at one-thirty in the morning was obviously a mistake on my part).

Valcareggi thought I was joking at first. When he realized I was serious he got very angry and ordered me back to my room. He said I was out of my mind to suggest such a thing, and that if I knew what was good for me I wouldn't tell anyone what we had discussed. And yet the next day he told team manager Italo Allodi and immediately the press found out. The northern papers were furious. Some Milan papers said I wasn't fit to play for the national team; others said I wanted to be the national team coach. Without wanting it I was the center of controversy (and this was before all the additional trouble stemming from my behavior during the Italy–Haiti game).

Of course, I wasn't the only one who fared badly during the course of the World Cup. There were so many angry fans waiting for Valcareggi and the team when we returned to Italy that our chartered plane to Milan had to go to Rome instead to avoid the thousands massed for retaliatory action at the airport.

My troubles lasted for months after the World Cup. It seemed as if all Italy was against me. Booing, whistling, and flying objects greeted me wherever I played other than at Olympic Stadium, where, thankfully, the Lazio fans were still on my side. Finally, a half year later, I was considered "rehabilitated," as the Italian press called it, and recalled to the Italian national team. However, the public wasn't as gracious or forgiving. In my first game since the World Cup, against Norway in Florence, I was booed from the time I entered the stadium until I scored in the second half. After that my reception did improve and I was generally accepted again by the Italian fans (although their acceptance was never more than lukewarm).

I also played two internationals in the spring of 1975. I was center forward against Poland when we tied, 0–0, in Rome. Italy's new coach, Fulvio Bernardini, the one-time famous attacking center half of Lazio in the twenties and thirties, picked Francesco Graziani, Paolo Pulici, and me as the strikers and for a while it looked as if Bernardini had found the right combination because we played much more attacking soccer than in the past. We were, however, never able to penetrate the strong Polish defense.

The other game was a 10–0 rout of the U.S. team in which Graziani scored three goals, I scored two, our midfielder Francesco Cordova scored two, and even our defender Francesco Rocca scored two. It was obviously a very one-sided game and you couldn't help but feel sorry for the young Americans as they wandered aimlessly around the field. Their team that day was Bob Rigby, Alan Hamlyn, Werner Roth, Dan Counce, Bobby Smith, Barry Barto, Dave D'Errico, Archie Roboostoff, Pat McBride, Andy Rymarczuk, and Paul Scurti; the subs were Buzz Demling, Kyle Rote, and Alex Skotarek.

As reigning champion a lot was expected of Lazio in the 1974–75 season but despite starting off very well we couldn't finish higher than fourth. Juventus won the championship again, Naples was second, and our archrival, Rome, much to our chagrin, was third.

The turning point for us was the illness of Tommaso. We were only four points behind Juventus when he went into a private clinic for tests. Once the seriousness of his illness became known we went to pieces. I remember well that sad afternoon when we found out exactly what was wrong with him. We were playing Turin and were losing, 2–0, at halftime. I called the clinic where Tommaso was being treated at halftime, and I was told that he had a cancerous tumor. The prognosis was that he had a few weeks to live (actually, he didn't die for another year).

We went out onto the field considerably demoralized and gave up three goals, losing, 5–1, the biggest defeat we had suffered since Tommaso's arrival in 1971.

Tommaso's illness took most of the joy out of soccer for me. I couldn't imagine Lazio or Rome without him. Tommaso and I had spent more time together than we had with our families. I had frequently gone home with him after practice and stayed there until Connie called and asked me to come home. An important part of my life would soon be lost and I was depressed about it.

It was while I was feeling low that Connie and I again discussed moving to America. As I said before, we had first seriously considered moving when we visited the United States in 1973. Connie had wanted to remain with her family and friends even then, but I convinced her in the end that the only realistic choice we had was to stay where I could earn a good living playing soccer: in Italy. But now we had good enough investments to be self-sufficient without an income from soccer. Connie felt that now was the time to buy property in the United States even if I could not live there with her and the children during the soccer season for several years. She pointed out that if I chose I could commute back and forth from Rome. Connie was shrewd enough to realize that real estate prices were beginning to skyrocket in America. Who knew, she said, what astronomical heights they would reach if we waited to purchase a house until I retired from soccer in 1982 or '83?

I had always looked forward to settling down in America eventually but I hadn't thought of doing it so soon. Nevertheless, I had to agree with everything Connie said, particularly her opinion about the changing real estate picture. I had been fascinated with the country in 1972, especially with the seemingly endless freedom Americans had to do just about anything they wanted to do without government interference. I know that a great many Americans feel they have too much bureaucratic involvement in their private lives but compared to Italy it is tiny, particularly for businessmen. Trying to make sense of the thousands of Italian laws on investments and taxes can drive you up the wall, as can the petty government officials, whose only function appears to be to come up with ways to block any ambitious business venture.

In April 1975 Connie and the children went off to the United States to stay with her family for a while as they had done several times before. But this time they would not be returning to Rome—Connie and I finally agreed to buy a house in America. Within a week she had purchased the house we now live in. Acquaintances who don't know Connie well ask me how I could give my wife the enormous responsibility of selecting our very first house without my seeing it. Well, it's simple; I have complete faith in Connie's judgment on everything domestic, from the choice of my clothes to the furniture in my study. After all, Connie was an art student and has always had a discriminating eye for beautiful things. I knew even before I saw our house that it would be exactly the type of house I had longed for all my life: beautiful yet comfortable.

Once the 1974–75 season was over I came to spend the summer at my new home and I was in seventh heaven. One day as I was relaxing near the pool I got a call from Peppe Pinton. He introduced himself as a consultant to the Hartford Bicentennial soccer team and asked if I would be available to play as a guest for his team against the Polish national team the following Saturday—only four days away. I thought it was a farfetched request and I chuckled a little before saying that it was out of the question, since even if I wanted to play my club, Lazio, would never have given its approval.

Even in those days Peppe was a persistent son-of-a-gun. He talked at length about how everyone would benefit from such a guest appearance: the American soccer fans would get to see me; I would get the chance to score against the Poles for the first time; and the Hartford club would be certain to draw its first big crowd. He also had the gall to add nonchalantly, "And don't worry about Lazio, Mr. Chinaglia. I will arrange everything."

Again I laughed. Anyone who knew Lazio's president Umberto Lenzini could have told Peppe that negotiations with him over the smallest matter could take weeks. I told Peppe his chances to arrange a deal with Lenzini within four days were nil.

"Well, at least let me come and talk to you," Peppe said.

Why not? I thought. I had this enormous house and lots of attractive new furniture that I wanted to show off to someone, so I said, "Okay. Come to my house and we'll have a drink and see what we can do."

Next morning Peppe chartered a small plane and flew in from Hartford (an experience which frightened him so much that he refused to fly back and rented a car instead). We talked for three hours; we discussed the coming game with Poland, exchanged views on Italian soccer, and reminisced about Italy. (Peppe was a native of Catanzaro and had come to study for a master's degree in the United States. He was now married and living in Hartford.) After we talked awhile Peppe called Lazio. I sat there smiling to myself waiting for Lenzini's outburst. But it never came. Within minutes the smooth-talking Peppe had Lenzini agreeing to everything. The only stipulation was that Hartford would have to take out a $2 million insurance policy on me before Lazio would give official permission for my guest appearance.

On that Friday Lazio gave its blessing. Hartford called a press conference to announce that I was to appear and that the game had been rescheduled for the following Sunday so that they would have another day for publicizing the game.

Peppe called that same day and asked if I could come to Hartford at noon on Saturday. I agreed and the next day he showed up in a borrowed Mercedes limousine and drove me back to Hartford. Peppe and the Hartford club were thankfully now getting the support of the local news media so there was a big turnout of reporters and TV crews. According to Peppe, the Hartford club had never been able to stir up much interest in the game until that Friday. Up to Monday of that week only 1,000 tickets had been sold and the event was destined to be a financial disaster since the Polish team was to receive a $30,000 minimum. In desperation, Hartford had asked Peppe for some ideas on how to drum up more interest. After a sleepless night without any solid ideas, Peppe heard from a friend that I had been seen in a New York restaurant. If Chinaglia would play, he told the Hartford owners, it would mean at least another 6,000 paying fans from Hartford's large Italian–American community. They agreed to his asking me and he spent all day Monday trying to track me down. Finally he reached a business associate of mine, who, after listening to his explanation of the difficult situation at Hartford, gave him my unlisted telephone number.

Peppe's week-long efforts paid off. There were 10,746 fans at the game—a record crowd for the Hartford team. Interestingly enough, before the game there were thousands of Italian–Americans waiting outside the stadium who wouldn't buy tickets until they were certain that I was going to play. When our Mercedes arrived they all cheered and then there was a mad stampede for the ticket booth with people pushing and fighting for a good place in the hastily formed lines.

I thought Hartford played extremely well against the Polish national team. It was an exciting game and although we lost, 2–0, we held our own and had as many opportunities to score as the Poles did. I should have scored in the first 10 minutes when I got a chest-high ball on a cross from Kevin Walsh, a young American. I moved it with my chest to my right, then hit a hard shot which went inches over the crossbar. Later I thought I had made up for that miss with a zooming shot that beat Jan Tomaszewski, the Polish goalie, but the goal was disallowed. Referee Gino D'Ippolito ruled that I was offside. (Yes, the same man who disallowed my goal against Argentina.)

After the game we went to an Italian–American club. A convoy of cars followed us and we were preceded by a police motorcycle escort with sirens blaring. The club was mobbed. It seemed as if everyone associated with the game was celebrating having done his bit for soccer in Connecticut.

The summer of 1975 was momentous in American soccer history because Pelé signed with the Cosmos. His first game for the team, then still called the New York Cosmos, was against Dallas. I didn't have tickets for the match so I called Clive Toye, then president of the club, and he graciously invited me to be his guest. During the game I mentioned to Clive that I wasn't going to return to Italy and that I would like to play for the Cosmos. He was interested and suggested that I come to his office the following day to discuss the matter.

The next day, in the Warner building, Clive reiterated how much he would like me to play for the Cosmos that summer, provided that he could get permission from Lazio. He then took me upstairs to meet Steve Ross. The three of us had a friendly chat and by the end of it they had offered me a very attractive contract. It was now all up to Lazio.

Steve and I became friends very quickly. We spent many pleasant Sunday afternoons at Steve's Fifth Avenue apartment. We discussed soccer endlessly and Steve asked excellent questions about training, tactics, and trends in world soccer. I could tell he had been doing his homework on the Cosmos and on the sport in general. I was also impressed by his ability to absorb everything he heard quickly.

Steve loved to watch soccer games and two weeks after we met he took me with him to Rochester to see the Cosmos play. We were both up that day since it seemed that Lazio was going to allow me to play for the Cosmos permanently. I thought I had convinced the Lazio management that I was staying in the United States when I took out a full-page ad in the *Corriere Dello Sport,* an Italian sports magazine, explaining to the fans that I wanted to be with my family and that, although I deeply appreciated their kindness and loyalty, I had to say farewell. The ad had cost me $1,000 but I would gladly have paid five times that amount to get my message across to the loyal Chinaglia fans, particularly 21,000 who belonged to the various Chinaglia fan clubs.

Steve and I had been expecting to hear from Lenzini that day but we left for Rochester without receiving a call. When we arrived at the hotel in Rochester, Steve checked to see if a phone call or a telex message had been received from Lazio. None had, and since we had to leave for the game Steve arranged for an Italian waiter in the hotel to stay by the telephone in case Lazio called. He was given precise instructions. "Now listen carefully," said Steve, "if Mr. Lenzini, the owner of Lazio, calls and says Giorgio can play for the Cosmos I want you to hang up immediately, because your statement will be good enough for me and any court in America will support me with you as my witness."

We never received the expected call from Lazio and I often wonder what would have happened if the waiter had hung up before Lenzini had, in his customary manner, taken the chance to bargain for additional money or to renegotiate some clause in the contract to his advantage.

Needless to say I was very depressed, so much so that when Steve offered me a space in his private plane to the team's next game in Washington I excused myself. I knew I wouldn't have been good company.

Later on that summer Lazio finally gave Steve an answer —but not the one we had been expecting; they refused to allow me to play in America. Discouraged and uncertain of my future, I was extremely lucky to have a friend like Steve. All summer long he tried to cheer me up and even went so far as to offer me an office job at the Cosmos if I decided not to return to Lazio for the 1975–76 season. He also invited me frequently to go watch the Cosmos games with him. I accepted a few times but after a while I told him I couldn't watch anymore, for I had a tremendous desire to play and sitting in the stands was driving me crazy. Steve said he understood and didn't ask me again.

It was this enormous craving to play soccer again that made me decide to go back to Lazio for the 1975–76 season. I had to play again and once Lazio agreed to my going home once every three or four weeks for a four-day visit I decided to become a trans-Atlantic commuter.

Torn between my love for my family and my love for soccer, I wasn't certain if I was making the right decision in going back to Italy. Nine months was a long time and I couldn't guarantee that Connie or I could stand it. Connie was in tears when I left her and the children. Although she was dead set against my returning to Lazio she also understood that at that point I couldn't exist without soccer. My departure was sad; I couldn't help but feel guilty. I could only hope I was doing the right thing.

When I returned to Rome I was surprised by an incredible sight: there were 10,000 people waiting for me at the airport at seven in the morning, many of them fighting with the police who were only trying to keep them under control. Windows and doors in the airport lounge were smashed, as were some of the windows of the plane that brought me there. To get me out of the airport in one piece the police were forced to send a riot truck to the runway. Once I was aboard the truck it didn't stop until we were in downtown Rome. It was one time I didn't have to worry about going through Customs.

With dedicated (if overzealous) fans like those at the airport it was no wonder I had mixed emotions about returning to Lazio. I knew I would never again see such a loyal and loving group, but I also knew that eventually I would have to disappoint them and go back to America even if it meant not playing soccer anymore.

CHAPTER 8

ONE OF THE FAVORITE PASTIMES of soccer players is putting together various all-star teams. Whenever I'm on the road I while away many hours in my hotel rooms reminiscing about players I have played with or have seen in action. Sometimes I just concentrate on the best in Italy, other times on the best I've seen in England and Wales, and, of course, often on the ultimate team—the world's best ever. Let me give you my choices. If nothing else, it might stimulate some good conversation between halves.

For my best-ever British team of players I actually played with or saw from the age of 12 to the present I would pick:

Goalie:	Gordon Banks (*England*)
Backs:	George Cohen (*England*)
	Jackie Charlton (*England*)
	Bobby Moore (*England*)
	Terry Cooper (*England*)
Midfielders:	Nobby Stiles (*England*)
	Bobby Charlton (*England*)
	Ivor Allchurch (*Wales*)

Forwards: George Best (*N. Ireland*)
                  John Charles (*Wales*)
                  Denis Law (*Scotland*)

My all-Italian team would consist of players who were playing between 1966 and the present:

Goalie: Dino Zoff (*Juventus*)
Backs: Pino Wilson (*Lazio*)
                  Roberto Rosato (*Milan*)
                  Tarcisio Burgnich (*Inter*)
                  Giacinto Facchetti (*Inter*)
Midfielders: Romeo Benetti (*Milan*)
                  Gianni Rivera (*Milan*)
                  Luciano Re Cecconi (*Lazio*)
Forwards: Franco Causio (*Juventus*)
                  Luigi Riva (*Cagliari*)
                  Roberto Bettega (*Juventus*)

The following NASL all-star team includes only players who have participated in the NASL from 1976 on:

Goalie: Phil Parkes (*Vancouver*)
Backs: Carlos Alberto (*Cosmos*)
                  Bob Lenarduzzi (*Vancouver*)
                  Wim Rijsbergen (*Cosmos*)
                  Bruce Wilson (*Cosmos*)
Midfielders: Johan Neeskens (*Cosmos*)
                  Franz Beckenbauer (*Cosmos*)
                  Vladislav Bogicevic (*Cosmos*)
Forwards: Dennis Tueart (*Cosmos*)
                  Giorgio Chinaglia (*Cosmos*)
                  Pelé (*Cosmos*)

In my nineteen years of pro soccer I have watched or played with all the great players of modern soccer. Still, choosing a world all-star team of the 1960s and 1970s is a much more difficult task than an Italian, British, or NASL team. After all, there are about thirty countries that have to be considered major soccer powers among the 140-odd countries that belong to FIFA. What makes it even more difficult is that once you get past Pelé—who stands alone —any position has at least twenty or more candidates.

I should also mention before sticking my neck out that I'm not including any of the host of great players who predate my soccer years. That means I've omitted legendary names such as Silvio Piola of Lazio: Harry Hibs, the great English goalkeeper of the twenties; Leonidas da Silvia, the Brazilian center forward of the thirties; Mathias Sindelar, the Austrian center forward of the thirties; and Ricardo Zamora, the immortal Spanish goalie of the twenties and thirties. Nor am I considering the Argentinian forwards, Angelo Labruna and Adolfo Perdernera; Alex James, the Scottish wizard; Italy's Giuseppe Massa; Hungary's Ferenc Puskas and Sandor Kocsis; or Dixie Dean, England's record goalscoring center forward.

Some of the stars of the 1940s and 1950s were still playing when I started with Swansea but I don't think it's fair even to consider them for they were past their prime. Stanley Matthews, for instance, played against us at Swansea but by then he was 49 and obviously just a shadow of the man who was probably "Mr. Soccer" to the whole world between 1938 and 1955.

Here, then, is my world's best team:

Goalie: Lev Yashin (*Russia*)
Backs: Franz Beckenbauer (*West Germany*)
                Carlos Alberto (*Brazil*)
                Jackie Charlton (*England*)
                Giacinto Facchetti (*Italy*)
Midfielders: Nobby Stiles (*England*)
                Pelé (*Brazil*)
                Gianni Rivera (*Italy*)

Forwards: Garrincha (*Brazil*)
                  Alfredo Di Stefano (*Argentina and Spain*)
                  Bobby Charlton (*England*)

Reflecting on my world team choices, I would have to say that Lev Yashin was everything a goalkeeper should be: acrobatic, thoughtful, and with amazing anticipation. He was a big man and capable of dominating his goal area to such an extent that opposing forwards often thought he was invincible. After Yashin, my preference would be either Gordon Banks or Dino Zoff.

Carlos Alberto and Giacinto Facchetti would grace anybody's best-ever world team. Both were unbeatable in their prime and few wingers ever came through a game wanting to face them again. Giacinto was exceptionally tall for a world-class back, and he was also one of the fastest. He almost singlehandedly introduced the overlap along the wing, which has since become such an important weapon in any top back's repertoire. Carlos, on the other hand, is known best for the unhurried manner in which he steals the ball from his opponent. But there's more to Carlos than how intelligently he plays defense. His ball control is as good as the best forwards' in the world and his passing is perfect. With two backs like these any midfielders and strikers would receive all the support they'd need.

At center back I was so impressed by the strength and consistency of Jackie Charlton that he beats out the more aristocratic Bobby Moore. Jackie, the brother of Bobby Charlton, was probably one of the most underrated players in the world during his heyday. His tremendous heading ability was unrivaled, he was much faster than he looked and he tackled like a bulldozer. I can never remember his playing a game in which he wasn't in command of the center of his defense. He was rugged and extremely physical but it's exactly those qualities that are needed in a modern center back.

Behind Jackie I would place the sweeper par excellence, Franz Beckenbauer. Here is another case of a player who by himself devised a new way of playing his position. With lots of courage and innovation, he moved into the attack from way behind his wall of defenders. Today attacking sweepers are not uncommon, but there still isn't one comparable to the Beckenbauer of the early seventies. Franz can play anywhere on the field and still look every inch the world-class star he is. Like Carlos, Franz is capable of making the hard things look casual and elegant.

I'm certain I'll raise a lot of eyebrows by picking Nobby Stiles as one of my midfielders. Johan Neeskens, Romeo Benetti, and the fiery Scot, Billy Bremner, have all been passed over for Nobby, who probably was the most hated player in the world outside of England during 1966, when England won the World Cup. Little Nobby (he is only five foot six) was not so much a dirty player as he was the most ruthless tackler the game has seen. Whatever his reputation, I consider him the best defensive midfielder of modern soccer and I would want him on my team to counterbalance my other two midfielders, Pelé and Rivera, both of whom are very offensive minded.

Pelé spent most of his playing years as a striker, but with the advent of defensive soccer and so many defenders in the penalty area I would prefer having him begin his attacks from the midfield where he would have more time and room to get possession of the ball. Actually, during his prime Pelé couldn't have cared less how tight he was marked or how much space there was for him to take passes. With his remarkable speed and dazzling ball control, he was capable of destroying any defense regardless of how many defenders stacked the penalty area. There probably will never be another player who has as many skills: ferocious shooting, thundering headers, breathtaking dribbling, and superb passing. I know he would not only score goals for my all-star team but provide just as many for his teammates with his unselfish passing.

As for Gianni Rivera, I would simply say he was the finest midfield passer I have ever seen. In addition to his world-class ball skills and an ability to read the game like nobody else, his pinpoint passing had to be seen to be believed.

Up front on the right flank, Brazil's Garrincha has no rival for the position. No winger in the last twenty years could dribble like he could. The best compliment I can give him is to repeat what a British journalist said during the televising of the 1958 World Cup final, "Garrincha was as good as Stanley Matthews only faster." Despite a leg deformity he had fantastic speed, an amazing body swerve, and startling acceleration from a standing position. The "Little Bird" also scored many goals with his powerful shooting, and like his teammate Pelé soared to great heights when heading goals.

At center forward there can only be one man for me, the one player who rivals Pelé as the greatest player in soccer's history—Alfredo Di Stefano. Tall, elegant, and with amazing stamina, he spent much of his playing career in Spain with Real Madrid and led the Spanish club to five European Cup championships. From his center forward position he not only scored goals but also directed his team's offense. Like Pelé, his shooting was powerful and accurate and his ball control, heading, and passing were superb. On top of all this, Di Stefano was a born leader who was the dominating figure on any team. I know I could rely on him to get the most out of his distinguished teammates.

My final spot goes to Bobby Charlton. Not simply because he was the hero of my schooldays, but because he was one of the finest players in the world during the

1960s. I would prefer him in midfield but not wanting to move Pelé up front I would have to think of Bobby as he was in the late fifties and early sixties when he was the speedy and devastating left winger, before he moved back to the midfield position. In any case, Bobby's all-around ability enabled him to perform equally well as midfielder, winger, and even center forward with Manchester United and England. Bobby, who may have had the hardest shot in European soccer during his day, would enjoy himself playing in front of Rivera and Pelé and would (if this dream team were only possible) score a hatful of goals.

So there's my world team and I can already hear my friends asking about Eusebio, Luigi Riva, Sandro Mazzola, Rivelino, Jairzinho, Johan Cruyff, Kevin Keegan, Osvaldo Ardiles, Gerd Muller, and Wolfgang Overath. The list could be endless. All I can say is that I think my combination of strength and brilliance would be equal to any other team that could be named for the 1962–80 era. And just to insure that my team of different styles and personalities would be able to function properly and get the most out of its talents, I would have as my coach Tommaso Maestrelli.

The players greeted me with affection when I returned to Lazio from America. Old friends like Pino Wilson, Giancarlo Oddi, Lorenzo Garlaschelli, and Felice Pulici made me feel as if I had never been away. The members of the maintenance staff (the ground crew, the cleaning ladies, and the old men who cleaned the shoes and did other janitorial odd jobs around the club) were also happy to see me. I always had a special relationship with them. They considered me their spokesman whenever they felt they were being wronged by the club. They were also grateful for the money I used to disburse among them—money I got from begging a small sum from the players when they received bonuses.

One of the reasons I felt the players should share their bonuses with the workers was that I had never forgotten what it's like to be poor. My strong feelings about the workers caused some big arguments in the clubhouse because I would get angry with some of the Lazio players who were themselves products of poverty and resisted my suggestion that they be a bit generous now that they had some money.

I sometimes raised money for the maintenance workers in another unorthodox way. If we played poorly I would go around the dressing room and tell each player, "Okay, we were terrible out there today so you're fined 20,000 lire." There were many days when I was able to collect a tidy sum. Pino Wilson told me that after a bad game the players were scared to come into the dressing room, as much because of my expected tongue-lashings as because of my imposed "fines."

There were times when I would explode on the field too. Once I kicked Vincenzo D'Amico in the behind because I didn't think he was trying hard enough. It was a game against Inter-Milan and I suppose in a way it was kind of funny. The team as a whole had been playing poorly and when Vincenzo let Sandro Mazzola waltz past him without chasing him I finally saw red. I took after Mazzola myself as if to give Vincenzo a demonstration of all-out effort when, much to my embarrassment, Mazzola pushed the ball through my legs and casually went on his way. Having fallen for the oldest trick in soccer I did look like a fool. I didn't like it much when Vincenzo just stood there and laughed. After the game, when both of us had cooled down, Vincenzo admitted that a kick in the butt was a small price to pay for the rare privilege of seeing the look on my face when the ball went through my legs.

I should add that, although the players often resented

my badgering them for money and my authoritarian manner both on and off the field, they also knew that whenever they needed help I would speak up for them with either Lenzini or Tommaso, for just as is true with the Cosmos now I was never afraid to speak my mind at Lazio. Honor and principles come first with me and I don't care what impression I make on people. It is true that I was often straightforward to the point of rudeness. I guess my teammates forgave me for that, as well as for my impatience with mediocrity, because I had several traits which offset them. All of them knew that my word is my bond and that I'm loyal—once I've made a friend he's always a friend no matter how far removed our lives become.

Giulio Corsini had become Lazio's new coach during my absence. He had replaced Tommaso, who was seriously ill. I didn't like Corsini from the beginning and he didn't like me. I suppose our personalities were too strong to blend well. I didn't have much respect for him either. He was a coarse individual, as far as I am concerned, and a complete flop when it came to running a soccer team. We argued a lot and occasionally came to blows. (The two of us were probably pretty funny to look at together; he was a very small man and I towered over him.) As a matter of fact, we had a fight the very first day of training. The trouble began when he greeted me with the news that I wasn't going to play in that evening's Italian Cup game. At first I was calm. I said, "Okay, you're the coach. I can't make you play me, but you had better go out and tell the fans." Outside there were 20,000 fans who had pushed their way into our small private training ground to see Lazio practice, and he knew why they were there: to see me.

Next thing I knew he had broken a bottle and threatened to hit me over the head with it. I stood there laughing at him until he left the dressing room still carrying his weapon.

I had been told that Corsini was slightly crazy but even

if he hadn't been before, no one would have blamed him for going nuts the way our team played during the next several weeks. Corsini lasted only ten weeks in all but that two-and-a-half-month period was a nightmare for Lazio. We kept losing our road games and tying our home games. The more games we lost, the more he picked on me.

I particularly remember the day of the Lazio–Rome Derby. We had gone into *ritiro* three days before the Sunday game, and on the first day I mentioned to Corsini that I was leaving for New Jersey on the following Monday.

"You're not going to America while I'm coach!" he said vehemently.

I argued with him but he was adamant. I felt betrayed for the management's approval of my commuting to New Jersey once every three or four weeks had been the main reason for my agreeing to return to Lazio. I ran off the practice field to the privacy of the dressing room. It had been a month since I had seen my family, and, being a very emotional person, I started crying.

My teammates found me still sobbing when they came back from practice. We had always been a very close team, almost like brothers. Of course we argued at times and even came to blows during moments of passion. But deep down we were protective of each other. The sight of me crying by my locker upset all of them and they turned on Corsini with a vengeance, yelling at him that he was trying to destroy the Lazio team. They demanded that he let me go to New Jersey but Corsini, who seemed to enjoy getting the players so upset, simply told them not to interfere in matters that didn't concern them.

The argument continued for some time. Some of the club directors even joined in. Suddenly all three sections of the team—the directors, the coach, and the players—were exchanging blows. Too upset to think clearly, I joined in and remember connecting with a good punch at someone's head and wondering who it was I had hit. It was really a ridiculous brawl and I think we all realized it for within thirty minutes everyone had made up (as we always did at Lazio); everyone, that is, but Corsini. He just wasn't the friendly type.

We didn't play well that Sunday in what turned out to be the usual tense and dirty game. We were losing, 1–0, until 15 minutes from the end when I scored the equalizer and, as was my custom when scoring against Rome, ran across to their side of the field and stood there grinning while they booed their hearts out. I was lucky enough to score many goals against Rome in Derbys, and such sweet goals they were! My memories of those occasions are still so fresh that closing my eyes I can hear the roar of the Lazio fans drowning out the groans, boos, and angry hissing of the Rome supporters. Such moments are meant to be savored.

After the game the players told Corsini that now he had to let me go since I had earned the team a point. This time Corsini made no comment so I assumed his silence meant I could go. I left the next morning and never heard any more about not being allowed to commute.

But despite having no more difficulty over visiting my family once every three weeks I was becoming increasingly depressed because I didn't like living away from them. Even when Tommaso was brought back from his convalescence to replace Corsini I was still unhappy. The sight of Tommaso, now thin and frail, made me sadder. He had supposedly made a remarkable recovery but actually was much sicker than anyone knew and managed to hold out only seven weeks before having to return to the clinic.

When Tommaso took over, Corsini made many statements to the press in which he blamed me for his dismissal and accused me of having too much authority on the club (shades of "Chinaglia runs the Cosmos!"). In spite of what he said, I hadn't wanted the club to fire Corsini. I felt sorry for him. He had had an impossible task trying to fill the idolized Tommaso's shoes. Because I realized this from the very beginning I tried to help him by suggesting ways he could improve his relations with the team members, but he stubbornly refused to listen to any advice. (In this respect he was very much like Eddie Firmani.) One afternoon after one of his stormy meetings with the players I said to him, "If you want to do well with Lazio you must try to understand the players' personalities."

He brushed this suggestion aside with his usual curtness. "I have my own way of doing things."

By the end of his tenure at Lazio I wasn't the only one who felt sorry for him; the whole team had become sympathetic to the tough situation he was in. We all felt particularly bad about the unfair treatment dealt him by the Lazio fans. They couldn't have cared less that our poor showing was mainly due to the fact that we were demoralized—they blamed it all on Corsini's coaching. I remember the night we traveled back to Rome from Ascoli where we had lost, 2–1. Our bus was accompanied all the way home by busloads of fans chanting "Corsini go home" the whole time. Sometimes it was frightening the way the fans turned on him once we began to lose. I know all of the players, no matter how much they resented him personally, were sorry to see him lose his job after such a short time. He did, after all, have a wife and family to support. If only he could have learned from his Lazio experience! But he didn't. He was hired by Cesena and fired there too. Later on he coached a second-division club (Bari) and after three months he was dismissed again for the same reason.

Meanwhile I was having my own problems. My life had become very unpleasant. The strain of living apart from my family added to the problem of being continually besieged by fans pleading with me not to leave Italy plus the nuisance of having to put up with the behavior of opposing fans, most of whom had never forgiven me for my poor World Cup performance and hated my guts even more when they learned I wanted to leave the country. All of it was taking its toll; I was a nervous wreck.

By March 1976 I no longer cared what people thought. All I wanted was to go home to New Jersey. I was the highest paid player in Italy and, I don't mind repeating what was commonly said at the time, more popular in Rome than the Pope (his activities were reported on Page 3 in the newspapers and mine were on the front page), but I was more than willing to give up both the fame and the luxurious lifestyle if Lazio would only release me from my contract.

Out of desperation, I told Umberto Lenzini that even if I didn't play soccer again I was leaving at the end of the season and never coming back. Lenzini replied that he would never release me from my contract if I left and I would never be able to play soccer again.

"If you want to be stupid go ahead and get FIFA to ban me," I yelled at him. "But if you want to make some big money for the club sell me now to the Cosmos."

I could see Lenzini had realized I wasn't bluffing so when I left his office I called Steve Ross and told him, "You must come over here and talk to Lenzini. If I don't come to America soon I will finish up in a mental hospital!"

Steve promptly sent over Clive Toye and happily Clive had a good meeting with Lenzini for Lazio agreed to sell me. However, Lazio was not willing to set a date.

Over the next three weeks I met many times with Lenzini hoping to persuade him to release me by the middle of April. Tommaso, despite his pain and fading strength, called Lenzini constantly to plead my case. Tommaso had been in favor of my going to America from the very beginning, and his support had much to do with Lenzini's finally becoming accommodating.

One day Tommaso called me and said, "Giorgio, I think the time is ripe for you to get the Cosmos to come back to see Lenzini."

I called Steve immediately. Three days later he sent Rafael de la Sierra and Norman Samnick, the Cosmos' lawyer, and the legal transactions were completed without any fuss. Lazio received $750,000 and I was willing to sign the contract for as little as a $30,000 bonus fee in order to get to America and my family. However, the Cosmos more than made up for my small share at that time. It was and still is the most generous club in the world.

All that remained was to find a way to avoid the thousands of fans who had threatened to stop my leaving. I decided I would slip out of town after the next game against Turin.

When Monday morning the day of my departure arrived, I was informed by the Roman police that there were thousands of fans at the airport threatening to prevent my Air Italia plane from leaving the runway. I was forced to go to a small airfield and charter a private plane to Genoa. From there I flew to Paris to board an Air France flight to New York.

I can still remember the indescribable feeling that overwhelmed me when I landed at J. F. Kennedy Airport; it was probably the same marvelous emotion that all immigrants feel upon coming to America, but it hit me doubly hard for not only had I arrived in the land of freedom and opportunity—I had come home as well.

CHAPTER 9

OUR MANY LONG SEPARATIONS during the 1975–76 season made me appreciate my family more than ever. That's why the summer of 1976 was one of the happiest periods of my life. I was home and enjoying every moment of it. In the beginning every day was like a holiday and I'm afraid I spoiled our children terribly until Connie put a stop to it. As for Connie and me, we were like newlyweds.

One nagging worry clouded the picture: I was concerned about how well I would fit in with the Cosmos or, rather, how well I would get along with Pelé, for in 1975 the Cosmos were Pelé. At Lazio I was considered the star attraction, the man around whom the team was built; at the Cosmos Pelé, at 36 still the number one figure in world soccer, was king and everyone else was subordinate.

I had realized all along that going to the Cosmos meant playing second fiddle because there was no way I or any other soccer player could replace Pelé. It didn't matter because I didn't ever want to topple him. The honor of being Pelé's teammate has been given to only sixty or so players in the world, and for me it was enough just to play alongside such a master. In fact, I was as excited as a teenager at the prospect of becoming a part of his world. My admiration for Pelé began when as an 11-year-old I watched him explode on television onto the international scene in the 1958 World Cup in Sweden. Later on I saw him play many games for Brazil, including those of the 1970 World Cup when he and his Brazilian teammates treated the world to a rare exhibition of modern attacking soccer the likes of which probably won't be seen again. Not that Brazil with its unlimited talent couldn't produce another team as masterful as the 1970 squad, but because it's unlikely they would produce another genius so exciting to watch as Pelé was in his prime.

When I showed up for my first Cosmos practice session Pelé greeted me like a long-lost brother, even though we had only met nine or ten times before. My nervousness over our new relationship vanished as soon as he embraced me and said, "I am very happy you are to be with us. We will have a great team now."

How can anyone not love him? I warmed to him from the first. And, even though I must admit we had our differences of opinion during our team's crisis in 1977, I never lost my deep reverence for him.

After Pelé's warm welcome he took me around the locker room and introduced me to the players, some of whom I had seen play in 1975 when I had watched a few Cosmos games.

There were three newly signed players from England: midfielder Terry Garbett, winger Tony Field, and center back Keith Eddy. All were from the English first-division club Sheffield United, a natural choice for our coach Keith Furphy to lure talent from as it had been his home prior to his Cosmos contract. I knew a lot about all three since I had kept a tab on English soccer while in Italy, and I was pleased to see players of their caliber joining the club. Two other new Cosmos arrivals whose presence impressed me were well known British stars David Clements, the former Everton and Irish international midfielder, and Charlie Aitken, who had played 560 games for Aston Villa. Adding Latin skills were two former Santos teammates of Pelé: Ramon Mifflin, the Peruvian international midfielder, and Nelsi Morais, a fast defender with the skills of a forward. There were also three top Americans: goalie Bob Rigby, Werner Roth, and Bobby Smith. Other players included the clever English forward Tommy Ord; Scottish defender Charlie Mitchell, a NASL veteran for seven years; Mike Dillon, a defender who had played for Tottenham Hotspur in England; Brian Tinnion, another English striker; and Brian Rowan, a Scottish defender.

At first glance, the team looked strong enough to beat all the others in the NASL. But it wasn't long before I discovered that the Cosmos weren't the only team that had reinforced their squad in 1976. Replacing the many British third- and fourth-division players who at one time composed 90 percent of the NASL playing personnel were many former English internationals such as Rodney Marsh and Tommy Smith (both at Tampa Bay), Chris Lawler (at Miami), Bobby Thompson (at Connecticut), Bob McNab and Bobby Moore (at Hawaii), and Geoff Hurst (at Seattle). There were also some fine Scottish internationals joining clubs in 1976: Eric Martin (Washington), Jimmy Robertson (Seattle), and Charlie Cooke (Los Angeles). In addition, big Mike England, the Welsh international, had arrived at Seattle, and the former European Player of the Year and Northern Ireland international Georgie Best was at Los Angeles.

These and other new players suggested that the Cosmos wouldn't have everything their own way in 1976. And we didn't, for by the time I played my first game on May 17 against Los Angeles the Cosmos had already lost two of their five games. We may have been one of the best teams in the NASL on paper, but in actuality we were only a little above average because our performances throughout 1976 were inconsistent, anywhere from terrific to ordinary. When we were on, we gave NASL fans a look at what top soccer is all about; when we were bad, we embarrassed the fans as much as we did ourselves.

Fortunately for me, my debut for the New York Cosmos (as the club was then called) was on a day when my teammates looked every inch the star players they were. Although facing a strong Los Angeles team headed by Georgie Best and Charlie Cooke, we were in complete command all through the game and won by a score of 6–0.

I scored two of the goals, as did Keith Eddy (both from penalties) and Pelé. The most heartening aspect of our performance was the marvelous way Pelé and I played together during the game. Los Angeles never knew which one of us to double-team and was confused by the way we each made space for the other. After the game Pelé was gracious enough to say that having me on the field made his job much easier. So much for all those critics who had been saying there was not room for both of us on the same team. As for the fans' opinion, the 24,000 at Yankee Stadium gave Pelé and me a standing ovation when we left the field together. I still consider that 6–0 win to be the best display by the Cosmos since I joined them.

I scored two more goals in my second game for the team when we beat Boston, 2–1, in Boston. Boston was a team which greatly impressed me. Sadly, the team was broken up later in the season when financial problems caused it to sell its top players—Wolfgang Suhnholz, the ex-Bayern Munich star; Tony Simoes, the Portuguese international; Ade Coker, the Nigerian striker; and Shep Messing, the American-born goalie who would join us in New York a few weeks later.

I later learned Boston's financial situation was not unique. Many clubs had inadequate funds. For every Cosmos there was a Rochester, for every Tampa Bay there was a Miami, for every Minnesota there was a Toronto, and for every Portland there was a Team Hawaii. And even in 1980 there are clubs holding on by the skin of their teeth because of undercapitalization.

It took me a few games to get used to my Cosmos teammates and I know it was more than a few games before they grew accustomed to my pregame silent ritual in the locker room. There were many curious stares as they watched me sit by my locker clearing my mind before performing the "Chinaglia Shoe Show." For years I have had the habit of not talking to anyone during the 30-minute period (sometimes an hour if I'm very tense) prior to a game. The last 10 minutes I spend inspecting my shoes, touching, bending, and rubbing them, and inserting new shoelaces. No matter how new, the shoelaces must be replaced. All this may sound like superstitious rubbish to the nonathlete, but I can't tell you how many soccer players have their own idiosyncrasies. (For instance, Franz Beckenbauer never shaves before a game, Georgie Best refuses to tuck in his shirt while playing, and goalie Dave Jokerst of the California Surf never plays unless he has one or more stuffed animals resting in the back of the net.)

After just two games I left the Cosmos for a twelve-day stay (four days of training and eight days of playing) with Team America. As a part of the 1976 Bicentennial celebrations the United States Soccer Federation (USSF) had invited the full national teams of Brazil, England, and Italy to join Team America in a ten-day tournament. It was an optimistic choice on USSF's part for these three were among the best teams in the world. Our chances of victory were slim even though Team America did include many former internationals.

Team America's first game on May 23 was against Italy in RFK Stadium in Washington. There were a great many Italians among the 43,000 spectators. They booed me when they saw me wearing the American uniform. The

Italian players were even more unfriendly. I was very surprised at the hostility of both the Italian fans and players since the Bicentennial tournament was supposedly just a festive celebration and not an official international.

We lost, 4–0, partly because Rodney Marsh and Georgie Best wouldn't play for us. Without them we lost whatever remote chance we had of beating the strong Italian squad, most of whom had been my teammates eleven months earlier when I had played my last game for Italy against Finland.

In Seattle we faced the talented Brazilians and fared better, only losing 2–0 before 20,000 fans. As a matter of fact, it was a 1–0 game until Roberto scored in the last minute of play.

Kevin Keegan scored two goals and Trevor Francis one when we lost to England, 3–1, in Philadelphia in the final game. Only 16,000 fans showed up, a disappointing crowd considering that England was the best team in the tournament. Brazil won the tournament trophy with a 1–0 victory over England, but I thought England and Italy played better soccer than the South Americans.

For a team hastily brought together Team America did a creditable job, particularly in its last two games. Against England we had been unlucky not to have scored two or three more goals. Ray Clemence, the classy English goalie, was fortunate to get a hand on a thunderous free kick by Pelé. We were also unlucky not to be awarded a penalty when Julie Vee was fouled just on the edge of the penalty area after a brilliant length-of-the-field dribble. I came close with an overhead scissors kick which beat Clemence but was kicked off the line by an English defender. Incidentally, there were six Cosmos players on the team which played England: Bob Rigby, Bobby Smith, Keith Eddy, Dave Clements, Pelé, and me.

After eight days of competition for Team America in three different cities, we returned to New York to face a

Cosmos schedule that included three away games: Tampa Bay on June 6, Minnesota Kicks on June 9, and Portland Timbers on June 12. I got tired just looking at the schedule.

I felt even more exhausted after the Tampa game. We were outclassed from the beginning to the end, losing 5–1. Tampa, which had won the 1975 NASL championship, had many quality players and worked extremely well as a unit. There were few spectators in the record Tampa crowd of 42,611 who could imagine any other team in the NASL but Tampa winning the 1976 championship. The Rowdies' forward line was as good as I had been told. Rodney Marsh and three other former English first-division players—Derek Smethurst, Clive Best, and Stewart Scullion—had been dubbed "Murderers Row" by some journalistic brain and there was little doubt the four of them murdered the Cosmos on that humid afternoon. Worst of all, our terrible performance was seen on national television.

Yet the Cosmos could still draw record crowds even if we did play brilliantly one day and poorly the next. At Minneapolis we were welcomed by 46,000, the second league attendance record set in our last two games. This time we won, 2–1, and the marvelous Minnesota crowd gave both teams a standing ovation as the game ended.

We didn't break a league record when we visited Portland but that was because the Portland stadium could only hold 33,000, and a capacity crowd was nothing new to that successful club. Before the full house we looked good and really did deserve our 2–0 win.

We then lost to Boston, 3–2, at home in a tiebreaker. Two days later we were scheduled to play again. (I could see trying to keep up with the busy NASL schedule, in which the league tries to get in a whole season of play in a few summer months, was going to take some getting used to.)

At least this time we were the hosts. The visitors were the Toronto Metro-Croatians. I had been told that no ethnic names were permitted in the league but soon learned that rules could be bent in the NASL, especially if a club threatened to close its doors if its name were changed.

We defeated Toronto, 3–0, with Bob Rigby magnificent in goal, earning his fifth shutout of the season. We had 18,000 spectators this time, a vast improvement over the dismal 7,000 for our last home game against Boston, but still surprisingly low considering that Pelé was so well liked in New York. I remember thinking at the time that perhaps the fans thought our team was not as good as our press releases made us out to be.

I had scored another goal, making a total of eight in seven games. I was now second in the scoring championship race, just behind Georgie Best; he had nine goals and three assists and I had eight goals and three assists. (In the NASL, unlike the rest of the soccer world, assists are counted as statistics. The NASL awards a point for each assist and two points for each goal scored so that the scoring championship does not necessarily have to go to the player who scores the most goals. But except for 1973, 1976, and 1979 it always has.)

At the end of June we lost two more games: a 4–1 drubbing at Chicago and a 3–2 loss at Washington. We played better at Washington than Chicago but I could see that despite having Pelé on the team we would have a difficult time just winning our division, let alone the Soccer Bowl.

A major barrier to our team's ever reaching its potential was a lack of team spirit (a problem that plagued the Cosmos for the next three years). Since our dogmatic coach, Ken Furphy, contributed to dissension on the team, I, for one, was relieved when he resigned on June 29. Furphy certainly knew his soccer but it didn't make up for what I believed to be his terrible weakness: an inability to get along well with other people. Gordon Bradley, who had been coach prior to Furphy's arrival in 1976 and was then vice president, returned as coach.

Gordon, unlike Furphy, was adept at handling personal problems. He was friendly and easy to like. Ironically, he turned out to be Furphy's opposite. Furphy's strength was Gordon's weakness. His knowledge of the game was just too limited. Nevertheless, he brought a more relaxed atmosphere to the club so it was not surprising that we began to win again. We won the next four games, including a 5–4 victory over Tampa Bay at home—sweet revenge for our 5–1 loss a month earlier. It was an entertaining and exciting game, as all Tampa–Cosmos games are, and the 27,000 fans in Yankee Stadium enjoyed every moment of the nine-goal thriller.

By beating Washington, 5–0, on July 18 we moved six points ahead of them in our Eastern Division. Our early season confidence had been restored by our recent goal-scoring spree and we were now confident of winning everything. Pelé was playing his best soccer since coming to the United States; our defense had improved beyond recognition; our new goalie, Shep Messing (recently purchased from Boston to replace the seriously injured Bob Rigby), was outstanding; and Ramon Mifflin, Dave Clements, and Terry Garbett had jelled into the best midfield line in the league. My doubts about getting into the play-offs had been premature. If we continued to play as we had since July began it was highly probable that Pelé would get his first NASL championship medal. One thing that worried me personally though was the fact that I hadn't scored for seven games in a row, a pattern I hadn't broken until I got one against Washington. I had been playing well enough but one in eight was a disgrace. Even in Italy I seldom went more than two games without scoring. I could only hope that I hadn't lost my touch.

We ended the season winning two and losing two. First Rochester beat us, 2–1. Then I scored a hat trick in a 4–0 defeat of Dallas and San Jose beat us, 2–1. Finally in our last game we destroyed Miami, 8–2. I scored five goals against Miami to tie the NASL record. (I also had two assists and the 12 points earned was a new NASL record.) Another record was set by Pelé with his four assists. He also scored two goals, one of which was probably the best goal yet seen in the NASL. He was facing away from the Miami goal and hit a cross from Tony Field with an overhead scissors kick that sent the ball whistling past goalie Gene Van Taylor at more than 60 miles per hour.

My five goals gave me 19 goals in 19 games. I now had a total of 49 points, four more than Derek Smethurst who finished in second place. Pelé was third with 44 points. I had won the scoring championship for 1976.

Despite how well we were playing at the end of the season, we were overtaken by Tampa Bay in the race for the Eastern Division title. Winning seven out of its last eight games, Tampa accumulated 154 points to our 148. Nevertheless, we knew we could beat the Rowdies if we met them in the playoffs. But before we could have that privilege, we first had to eliminate Washington in the first round (Tampa as divisional champion had a bye in the first round).

On August 17 we were easy victors over Washington with goals from Pelé and Terry Garbett. (In 1976 playoffs were just one-game contests.) Three days later we traveled to Tampa Bay for what we considered at the time would be the game to decide the eventual Soccer Bowl winner. Before 36,000 delirious Tampa fans Derek Smethurst scored within five minutes of the kickoff. Pelé headed in the tying goal just before halftime and during halftime we were confident that we would be able to score and win the game in the second half. And we might have but for our concern for Pelé, who in our opinion was viciously fouled by the tough English defender Tommy Smith. Demanding a free kick, we argued with the referee who wouldn't listen. Taking advantage of our momentary lapse, Stewart Scullion kept running with the ball and scored. We seemed to lose heart after that goal and the game, which up to that time had been closely fought, became a one-sided affair. Rodney Marsh put the game on ice with a beautiful goal, dribbling around two of our defenders before hitting the ball hard past Shep Messing.

Thus ended the 1976 season for the New York Cosmos as Tampa Bay went on to meet Toronto in the semifinals. Surprisingly, the Rowdies did not win the Soccer Bowl as most people thought they would. They ran aground against the tough and surprising Toronto Metro-Croatians, who went on to beat Minnesota in the Soccer Bowl.

Although we didn't win the championship or even the Eastern Division title in 1976 I was still very happy to be with the Cosmos. The club might not have attained top-class status or have found the best managerial staff yet, but the friendly atmosphere on the club was already far superior to anything I had encountered in Italy or Wales. No one knew better than we did that there was a lot of work to be done before the club was ready to face the top teams in the world, but I was confident after my discussions with Steve Ross, the Ertegun brothers, and Clive Toye that the Cosmos would be a powerhouse in international soccer within a few years.

The signs were there in 1977 that the Cosmos meant to get to the top in the shortest possible time. During the season two of the finest players in the world, Franz Beckenbauer and Carlos Alberto, came to New Jersey (we now played at Giants Stadium). There were also other distinguished arrivals: Vito Dimitrijevic, a splendid attacking midfielder from Olimpa, a Yugoslavian first-division club; Steve Hunt, a great little winger from Aston Villa in England; Jomo Sono, the speedy and clever striker from South Africa; and Erol Yasin, a Turkish international goalkeeper from Galatasaray, who would compete with Shep Messing for the goalkeeper spot.

Strangely, the addition of so much new talent did not change the fact that we were always ready to form splinter groups. There were those who loved Gordon Bradley and those who felt he was ineffective; those who supported Erol Yasin in goal and those who considered Shep Messing the best goalie in the country; those who felt the Warner executives were too often making the decisions for the Cosmos instead of the club's managerial staff and those who thought the managerial staff under Clive Toye was not equipped to take on the increased responsibilities that came with the better players the team got.

I tended to side with the Warner executives. Clive had done a fine job in his early years with the Cosmos, but since the arrival of Pelé I thought the Cosmos had grown too big for him. Many mistakes had been made in the front office in recent years: players had been bought and sold with alarming regularity. At the beginning of the 1976 season, for example, there were only nine returnees from the 27-man squad. Also, attendance had not justified the increasing expenditures, at least until the middle of 1977. Perhaps the most painful fact was that those enormous expenditures had not even won us a championship. (Our last had been in 1972. As a matter of fact, we didn't win another championship until after Clive had left.)

When Clive resigned in June everyone pointed their finger at me as the one responsible. Once again I found myself on the defensive, but all I had done was to express an opinion when asked. Yes, I had been asked by the Cosmos board for an appraisal of the club's administration, and of Clive in particular. As usual, I was straightforward and candid in my reply and told them that I didn't think he or the administration as a whole was functioning well in 1977. However, as I have said so many other times, I simply give opinions; it is the board that makes the decisions. In this case the board was unanimous about letting Clive go and replacing him with Ahmet Ertegun.

I know that Clive still feels I had him fired and I feel bad that he holds a grudge against me. Actually, I think Clive is one of the great names of American soccer and I still admire his tremendous contribution to the success of the game here. He would make a splendid commissioner of the NASL and I hope one day to see him guiding the league's fortunes. But I still believe I was right in my assessment in 1977, and that he was not the right man for the Cosmos at that time.

There was too much fuss made over the "Toye Affair." I believe the sporting fraternity in the United States tends to exaggerate the importance of soccer administrators. The managerial class may be all-important in American football or baseball, but not in soccer. In our sport the players are the vital element. Who is on the field is what really counts, not who is appointed president, general manager, business manager, or public relations director. Unless American clubs realize this fact and concentrate on getting talented and exciting players, all the millions now being channeled into soccer franchises will be money wasted. Sophisticated and exciting soccer is what the public is interested in and the players who provide this can be had. But only for good salaries. I would like to see more emphasis on providing decent salaries for all NASL players and less on maintaining expensive NASL executives.

There was an uneasy atmosphere in and around the Cosmos locker room during that early part of the 1977 season. Arguments among the players were commonplace. Even Pelé and I had angry words despite our mutual admiration. For example, at one team meeting when we were discussing the team's inability to win against inferior teams, he said I was to blame because I was shooting too much. I replied that I was shooting because I expected to score and that scoring was more difficult than it should be because he was playing so close to me that his marker was able to mark me as well. We were playing 4–2–4 at that time and with Stevie Hunt and Tony Fields out on the wings Gordon Bradley had put both Pelé and myself in the middle. I had felt all along that Pelé should never have been given a position on the field but that he should have been allowed to roam at will while the rest of us supported him. Pelé needed room to do his magic. It was so obvious that his incomparable talent was being wasted in the penalty area with defenders marking him tightly and working him over physically.

Furphy's ideas about Pelé's role on the field were just as bad. I remember one game when he had insisted Pelé play on the left wing, which was really ridiculous.

Disturbed by all this bickering, I went into a slump. I couldn't score goals and I wasn't doing much to help the other forwards score either. Although I felt Bradley's poor tactics were partly to blame and that my teammates were also playing below their capabilities I still felt miserable in those first few months of 1977.

Most soccer players go through slumps but for a striker it is immeasurably worse than for a midfielder or a defender for the striker soon begins to panic and shoot whenever the ball comes near him, no matter how outrageous the angle, how high off the ground the ball, or how awkward the bounce. He no longer has the three important characteristics an experienced striker must possess: coolness under attack, the patience to pass the ball until he can get better position, and the willingness to run without the ball in order to make space for his teammates. Sadly, the more he fails to score when he shoots, the more distraught he becomes until finally he is of no value to his team.

My slump was a frightening experience. I was worried that top-class soccer might be over for me. I was so demoralized that I began to ask myself whether I wanted to make the effort to keep my place on the team. I actually considered retiring. Thankfully, Connie and many of my friends rallied around me and argued me to be patient. Jim Karvellas, the radio and TV personality, was more direct with his counsel: "Stop feeling sorry for yourself, Giorgio. You're letting your critics destroy you. Now stop acting like a young rookie and remember you are Chinaglia."

Gradually, my confidence came back and later, after my old friend Eddie Firmani was appointed coach, I was once again truly my old self. But I still shudder when I remember that early part of the 1977 season—a very gloomy springtime.

In our opening game at Las Vegas we played like a third-division team. It was a miserable performance and we deserved to lose by a bigger margin than we did (the final score was 1–0). Next we managed to defeat a poor Team Hawaii, 2–1, and we also beat Rochester, 2–0, in our first home game at Giants Stadium. The 26,000 home crowd was happy to see both Pelé and I get our first goals of the season that day. Neither of us scored in our 2–1 loss to Dallas in our next Giants Stadium appearance —this time in front of only 13,000 people. Our next three home games drew 20,000, 21,000, and 20,000 people, respectively. Finally, on June 5, the day of Franz Beckenbauer's home debut, we managed to get our first 30,000 gate. But even 30,000 was a disappointing turnout since the club had expected to double its 1976 average of 18,227 once Franz performed his magic alongside Pelé.

There had obviously been concern on the Cosmos' part over the slow increase in our home attendance ever since

Pelé's arrival in 1975. Pelé had no trouble attracting stand-ing-room-only crowds on the road but in New York in 1975 the biggest attendance was only 26,127. In 1976 it wasn't much better with a 28,436 high. And now in 1977 Franz Beckenbauer, the captain of the World Cup championship team of 1974, a truly great player, could only entice another 2,772 fans to the beautiful Giants Stadium with its easy accessibility, ample parking, and excellent view from any of its comfortable seats. If the Cosmos were going to continue to sign top international superstars, they certainly were going to need bigger crowds than the ones they were getting to help pay the club's annual multimillion-dollar payroll.

The reason why fans hadn't been knocking down the gates to get in to see us perform, of course, was because we had been playing uninspired, sloppy soccer. New York fans are probably the most sophisticated soccer fans in the country, and it didn't take much expertise to conclude that the 1977 version of the Cosmos was not performing any better than the inconsistent 1976 squad.

Fortunately, Beckenbauer's first home game (against Toronto) was the beginning of a five-game winning streak. It was also the game in which our offensive power finally came to life with six goals. This 6–0 rout was the answer to the Cosmos ticket office's prayer for our next home game against Minnesota brought in 36,816 fans and the following one on June 19, the phenomenal and com-pletely unexpected crowd of 62,394 to watch us defeat Tampa Bay, 3–1.

A few days earlier Clive Toye had resigned and Ahmet Ertegun had taken over as president. Next to go was our coach, Gordon Bradley. Replacing him was Eddie Fir-mani. A good deal has been written about my extensive role in Eddie's hiring so I'm delighted to surprise a few people with an account of my true contribution.

In February 1977 Peppe and I went down to Tampa to

train. We stayed at the Harbor Inn, a beautiful hotel conveniently situated alongside miles of golden beaches. Peppe and I worked out a training schedule which included a morning routine of a six-mile run on the beach, then calisthenics and ball control. In the afternoon we would go over to the Tampa Bay Rowdies for practice with the team. Eddie was still the Rowdies' coach so we saw him on a daily basis. It didn't take Peppe and me long to discover that he was unhappy in his position with the club. His authority had been weakened by the club's re-signing of Rodney Marsh, when everyone knew that Eddie didn't want the outspoken English star back. While we were there Eddie spoke on a number of radio programs and discussed how unhappy he was with Marsh's behavior the season before.

Knowing how he felt, Peppe and I often discussed with Eddie the possibility of his coming to coach at New York one day. But our conversations were all just talk, since at that time we had no idea that Eddie would be leaving the Rowdies three months later or that there would also be an opening at the Cosmos in 1979. There is no doubt, however, that when Eddie did resign from Tampa the Cosmos board became very interested.

In the middle of June, Steve Ross confided in me that the Cosmos were looking for a new coach. "Giorgio, I know you're a good friend of Eddie Firmani," he said, "but what do you think of him as a coach?"

"He's without doubt the best coach in the NASL," I replied quickly. I then went on to praise Eddie for the super job he had done at Tampa Bay and to explain why I thought he would do a good job at the Cosmos if he were chosen.

If you expected some cloak-and-dagger intrigue, I'm sorry but that's really all there was to my involvement in the decision to hire him. Believe me, if I had been a part of some undercover negotiations I certainly would not have gone around telling reporters and friends that I had recommended Eddie. But I must admit the accepted story showing me as the decision maker behind the scenes did make for better copy and, as I jokingly commented to a Roman TV reporter at the time, "In the NASL we are more than happy to get in the papers even if the stories are fabricated nonsense or outright lies."

Eddie's arrival had a real uplifting effect on the team. Within a few weeks we had resolved much of the petty differences, the constant bickering, and the inertia on the field that had plagued us all season. He moved Pelé back into the midfield, made Carlos Alberto the team's sweeper, and let Franz Beckenbauer tie up with Pelé in the midfield. He also gave Bobby Smith another chance to settle down as our right back, which Bobby did with outstanding success.

Almost three weeks after Eddie had assumed control we dazzled the soccer world with a sensational display of attacking soccer against Washington at Giants Stadium. In our 8–2 win Pelé, Steve Hunt, Tony Field, and I combined to produce some brilliant moves up front and behind us Franz Beckenbauer and Carlos Alberto strolled through the Washington players as if they weren't there.

The Washington game was definitely the turning point for me. There were two reasons why I had to regain my preslump form that day. First, the crowd thought I was responsible for Eddie's being hired and was expecting me to perform well for a coach I had supposedly hand-picked. Second, I had to prove I had known what I was talking about when I had made a certain comment to the press when Franz was signed. I had said, "What we need is an attacking midfielder, not another sweeper." The comment had caused a storm of protest from fans at the time, especially the German–American ones. Franz was now playing as an attacking midfielder so I wanted very much to convert his passes into goals to vindicate myself.

Setting objectives for myself has always worked well for me. Although outside forces had made me set a goal this time there was no difference in the result. I knew I had to produce, and I did. I got my first hat trick of the season and was in high spirits after a game for the first time that season.

We faced Tampa Bay in the first round of the play-offs. The winner of this game would then take on Fort Lauderdale, which had finished with 161 points to win the Eastern Division title. For the second straight year we had finished second but, unlike 1976, I was certain we could defeat our first-round opponent, Tampa Bay. Eddie went even further. "We're going to win the Soccer Bowl, make no mistake," he told us before the game.

The 57,000 fans at Giants Stadium saw a cautious first half in which both defenses dominated the play. It was not until midway through the second half when Pelé put us ahead, 1–0, that the fans really began to enjoy the game. Their roar of approval was deafening after Pelé's second goal and my first. Overnight, everyone seemed to have become a Cosmos booster. It was clear by the next morning that the Cosmos ticket office wouldn't have enough seats for all those who wanted to attend the Cosmos–Fort Lauderdale game on the following Sunday night. So it wasn't only Tampa Bay that could draw big crowds (62,394 and 57,191) to Giants Stadium after all. We were finally starting to draw record crowds on our own merits.

With 50,000 tickets sold in advance and hordes of vehicles approaching the stadium in spite of rainy weather it was obvious, especially to anyone trying to find a parking space in the 20,000-car parking lot, that a new NASL record was in the making that Sunday. But it was still a shock when the official attendance of 77,691 was flashed onto the enormous electronic scoreboard. Gaining 64,000 new fans in one season (from 13,000 in April to over 77,000 in August) would probably have inspired any team to go out and play super soccer; it certainly had this effect on us. It just happened that it was Fort Lauderdale that took the full impact of the red-hot Cosmos this day, but it could have been any other NASL team and the result would have been the same. It is difficult to single out any individual Cosmos player for special honors since everyone was outstanding. Nevertheless, I'm not going to let the opportunity pass, for Stevie Hunt was marvelous. He had a hand in six of our goals, including the two he scored. I scored another hat trick, Franz Beckenbauer got two goals, and Tony Field the eighth in our 8–3 win.

None of us had doubts anymore about our winning the Soccer Bowl. We went to Fort Lauderdale for the second game and beat them with a 3–2 shootout win. Then we defeated Rochester, 2–1, in Rochester and won the return game, 4–1, before 73,669 happy fans at Giants Stadium.

Our opponents in the Soccer Bowl would be Seattle, a team not to be taken lightly, for it had eliminated Vancouver, Minnesota, Dallas, and Los Angeles on its way to the final as well as beating us, 1–0, during the regular season. A hard-running team filled with former British first- and second-division players, Seattle was, as many critics reminded us, the type of team we had the most trouble handling.

The Soccer Bowl was held in Portland. Somehow 35,548 people crammed into the city's small Civic Stadium. From the moment the game started it was clear the fans were of two minds about whom to support. They all wanted to see Pelé end his career with his first NASL championship, yet they also wanted their West Coast team to whip the $10 million Cosmos.

It was hot and humid when we lined up on the afternoon of the game. The white-shirted Sounders had an impressive lineup: Tony Chursky, the Canadian international, in goal; Mel Machin, a NASL all-star; Dave Gillet, a tenacious, tall center back; Mike England, another NASL all-star and former Welsh international; Jim McAlister, the 1977 Rookie of the Year; Adrian Webster, a tough defensive midfielder; Steve Buttle, a goalscoring, aggressive midfielder; Jimmy Robertson, the speedy Scottish international winger; Jocky Scott, a clever Scottish forward on loan from Dundee of the Scottish first division; Tommy Ord, the former Cosmos forward who was now a consistent scorer with Seattle; and Micky Cave, Seattle's leading scorer.

Dressed in the Cosmos' green shirts and white shorts were: Shep Messing in goal; Bobby Smith, Werner Roth, Carlos Alberto, and Nelsi Morais on defense; Terry Garbett, Franz Beckenbauer, and Tony Field at midfield; and Pelé, Stevie Hunt, and me on the forward line.

From the opening kickoff the Sounders ran at us like express trains. We were under pressure for most of the first half from their long balls out of their defense to Ord or Cave and their nonstop running with or without the ball. It was very much against the grain of play when we scored the first goal of the game. I had passed a ball to Stevie Hunt only to have it intercepted by Tony Chursky. All of us moved back toward our goal as usual when the opposing goalie has control of the ball—all of us, that is, except Stevie. He stayed close to Chursky and when the Seattle goalie rolled the ball on the ground Stevie darted in, took it, and pushed it into the goal. Not looking behind him before he rolled the ball was a disastrous error on Chursky's part. We were so delighted by Stevie's surprising goal that we nearly choked him when hugging him. Pelé was so excited he lifted Stevie off the ground and held him up for the crowd to see.

The game was a long way from over, though. Four min-

utes later a beautiful quick classic give-and-go between
Mickey Cave and Tommy Ord ended with Cave blasting
the ball past Shep Messing to even the score.

At halftime Eddie did a little yelling about our lack of
drive and the way he kept looking at me I assumed I was
one of the main culprits. I felt like defending myself, explaining how well big Mike England (all six foot two of
him) was sticking to me, but the look in Eddie's eyes
warned me to keep quiet. Poor old Pelé looked most
unhappy. This was his last official game for the club and
he wanted to win it so much you could see the tears form-
ing in his eyes. (If you think I'm emotional you should see
Pelé when he's very sad or very happy.) One other player
who was upset was Terry Garbett. He had played a fine
first half, I thought, but Eddie told him he was out and
Vito Dimitrijevic, the Yugoslavian midfielder, was in for
the second half. Regardless of how sound a coach's thinking is when he makes a substitution in a championship
game it is agony for the man taken out. Terry had always
worked hard for the club and is one of the most likable
players. We all wanted to go over and console him, but I
think we realized that sometimes it is better to leave a
man alone with his disappointment.

The Sounders continued to run their hearts out in the
second half but the pace had slowed a little. We began
to move the ball around more intelligently and our midfielders were now opening up the Sounders' defense with
some fine passing outside their penalty area. Twice Pelé
came close to scoring from fine midfield passes. Then Stevie
Hunt picked up a pass out on the left wing. Chased and
buffeted by Mel Machin, he ran down the left wing and
somehow managed to cross the ball even though it seemed
Mel Machin's leg was blocking its passage. As the high
ball came over the goal area, I ran ahead of the Seattle
defenders and struck the ball with a flick of my head

sideways toward the goal at a 45-degree angle. As I made contact I knew it was a goal and I knew we had won.

I don't score many goals with my head so it seemed ironic that this vital goal, one of the most important of my career and the one that enabled us to give Pelé the championship we all wanted him to retire with, should have been a header.

There's nothing that can unite soccer players—or any team—more than a championship victory, and in the madhouse that was our dressing room after the game even our unemotional British players joined in the hugging and kissing. None of us associated with the Cosmos that day will ever forget the joyful scene as we celebrated not only a victory but also a strong team spirit.

A few weeks later another touching scene occurred when Pelé was the star attraction in "Pelé's Farewell" game. On October 1, 75,000 stood in the pouring rain at Giants Stadium to pay homage to the Black Pearl in his last Cosmos appearance. Out on the field flanked by his father, five former World Cup championship team captains, Professor Mazzei, Muhammad Ali, children in soccer uniforms, and TV camera crews from all over the world, Pelé gave his memorable farewell. With tears flowing down his face and his voice breaking repeatedly he finished with the message, "Love is more important than anything else in our lives. Please say with me three times, Love . . ."

And we all did. It was an unforgettable experience, a moment of American soccer history that will never be equaled in our lifetime. All of us on the Cosmos were honored to witness that touching event.

When the field was cleared Pelé was still wearing a Cosmos shirt but in the second half he planned to switch to the colors of our opponents, Santos, his only other club.

I can hardly remember the game itself I felt so drained

emotionally. Except for one brief period late in the first half nothing stands out in my mind. But that brief moment I'll never forget. Pelé had strolled up to take a free kick. The ball was about 30 yards from the goal, too far out to make the experienced Santos defense, which had set up a four-man wall, very worried. But they were wrong to underestimate the Black Pearl's capabilities; Pelé had not lost his touch and we were all about to see again why goalkeepers since 1957 have shaken in their shoes when Pelé takes free kicks. A couple of steps, a cocking of his right foot, and then a cracking sound as the ball flew into the net before Ernani, the Santos goalie, could move. It was the 1,281st and last goal of his career and it couldn't have been a better one. We won the game, 2–1, but what really mattered was the fact that Pelé had scored a goal in his last game.

At the end of the game he ran a lap around the field acknowledging the standing ovation of the soaking-wet fans. The electric scoreboard flashed "THANKS PELÉ" as he was carried off the field on the shoulders of Shep Messing and Erol Yasin.

We at the Cosmos still see Pelé regularly but for most of the American and international soccer fans watching on television Pelé said his last goodbye when he flashed that world-famous grin and disappeared into the Giants Stadium tunnel.

CHAPTER 10

AT THE BEGINNING of my third NASL year I was determined to score more goals than in 1977. It was about time, I decided, that I won the NASL's MVP award. When I had topped the goalscoring list in 1976 Pelé had won the trophy. In 1977 I was confident it was to be my year after I broke the playoff goalscoring record but Franz Beckenbauer edged me out.

In 1978 I did score more goals. As a matter of fact, I had my most successful season with the Cosmos and broke many NASL goalscoring records. Nevertheless, I was passed over when the MVP was awarded. (I was also to lose out in 1979 even though I think I could make a good case for myself.)

I hate to think I'm getting paranoid in my old age but I can't help thinking that there are people in the NASL hierarchy who have decided I will never get my hands on the MVP. Peppe is convinced that it's all Phil Woosnam's doing and he may be right. Certainly our relations have deteriorated ever since Woosnam turned down my bid for a NASL franchise in the fall of 1977.

The irony of my attempt to become a club owner was that I would never have thought of such an idea if Woosnam himself hadn't first suggested it to Peppe when the two of them were flying together to Rochester in the summer of 1977 for a Cosmos game. When Peppe told me about Woosnam's suggestion that I should consider having a franchise in the league I became very interested. Within a couple of months Peppe and I had found the necessary backers to provide sufficient capital for a sound club. We chose the city of Hartford for two reasons: Peppe knew it well and we felt we could draw sufficient crowds there to make a good return on our investment.

Peppe and I met with Woosnam at the La Grenouille restaurant in New York. After a pleasant meeting the commissioner instructed us to send in the application and a check for $25,000. It seemed then that we had a franchise, but soon afterward Woosnam told Peppe he would like to see more backing for our proposed club and a major company as the 51 percent majority stockholder rather than me. So Peppe went out and secured exactly what the commissioner asked for. But it didn't do us any good because our franchise bid was rejected. Peppe got a call from the commissioner who said that Houston had been awarded the franchise instead of Hartford. It was clear that he had been negotiating with several groups of backers simultaneously. As far as I'm concerned, his actions were underhanded because he had kept our check for weeks and had implied that we had met all the requirements for membership in the league.

In the summer of 1979 my relations with Woosnam got even worse after he sent me the following letter:

> Dear Giorgio,
>   No reply has been received to my letter of May 24 regarding your comments in the April issue of Sport

magazine. Therefore, for your actions you are hereby
fined one hundred dollars. Payment of this fine must be
made by personal check and received in the league office
by no later than Friday, June 15 or additional fines will
be imposed. Please understand that if it should be necessary to discipline you in the future for violations of
regulation section 9-4 stronger action will be taken.

Phil Woosnam
Commissioner

The letter made my blood boil. I stormed into Peppe's
office and flung the letter onto his desk. He read it hurriedly. "I told you he was going to make an example of
you!" was Peppe's comment. After a minute's reflection
he added, "Don't pay it."

"Who cares about the money, Peppe! I just think the
whole thing is ridiculous. Even in Russia you can make
statements to the press without being held responsible for
what they print."

"Don't worry, Giorgio, Woosnam's on his way out as
commissioner."

Peppe had been telling me this for nearly two years but
Woosnam's ouster still hadn't come about. Peppe was
convinced that the club owners felt Woosnam had served
his purpose by expanding the league but was no longer
the type of commissioner the office now required. What
they needed now, he said, was a high-powered executive
accustomed to operating the country's biggest corporations, someone capable of delegating the minor tasks while
he concentrated on solving the many problems now be-
setting the league. Peppe was certainly privy to the opinions of a good many owners, but I knew there were some
important ones who remained Woosnam's friends if only
out of gratitude for his successful efforts to transform a
once very unimportant NASL into a major sports league.
I doubted they would all desert him without a fight.

Well, he's still in office. I probably will be retired by the time he's finally replaced.

I make no bones about my great disappointment at not receiving the MVP award in 1978. I certainly don't want to belittle the fine performance of the eventual winner, Mike Flanagan, but I felt I had earned it with my 34 goals in the regular season and the five I collected in the playoffs.

Mike, who played for the New England Teamen while on loan from Charlton, the English second-division team, provided a tremendous challenge for me in our two-man contest for the goalscoring championship. Our race for the title began in earnest way back on May 7 when he scored four goals against Chicago. From then on both of us scored consistently in a neck-and-neck fight up to the final game of the season.

We had started off the season in 1978 beating Fort Lauderdale, 7–0, and thereby serving notice on all the other NASL teams that we intended to win our second straight NASL title. Bogie, making his first NASL appearance after coming to us from Red Star Belgrade, tied Pelé's record of four assists, and Steve Hunt and I both had hat tricks. It was a spectacular way to begin a new season, especially since we were now the Cosmos minus Pelé. The dire forecasts about what would happen to us once he was gone seemed to have been taken care of in just one game. Not only did we have a fine performance on the field but the 44,000 fans who came to Giants Stadium broke our opening day attendance record.

By the middle of May there was no doubt that the 1978 Cosmos were a far better team than the 1977 version. We had won the first seven games and had scored 24 goals in the process. We knew we were playing exceptional soccer when we visited Tampa and won our first

game there. It was a convincing 5–2 win. The addition of
Bogie, Dennis Tueart from England's Manchester City,
and my old friend Pino Wilson from Lazio had given us
a better defense, more power up front, and a more creative midfield. Although we had lost a game to Portland
on May 17 and were beaten by Memphis two weeks later,
there didn't seem to be any team in the league capable
of taking our title from us.

Before our Memphis defeat we had beaten Seattle,
5–1, in front of 71,000 fans at Giants Stadium and after
the Memphis game we won another seven games in a row,
including 5–1 victories over Rochester and Toronto and a
6–1 win over Washington. In addition to my opening day
hat trick, I collected one against Seattle and one against
Washington so that by June 19 I had collected 20 goals to
Mike's 14 and was a comfortable 17 points ahead in the
scoring chart with 48 to his 31. But by July 5, when we
traveled to New England, Mike had scored 22 goals to
my 24.

We lost to New England, 1–0, in overtime with Mike
(who else?) scoring the winner. On July 9 Mike equaled
the NASL record by scoring five goals in one game against
California. On July 12 the Teamen came to Giants Stadium and in front of 62,000 surprised fans beat us again
by a score of 3–1. Mike and I both scored a goal. He
now had 29 to my 26.

Despite our double loss to the Teamen, we were 41
points ahead of Washington in the Eastern Division·with
only seven games to go. Now we had another winning
streak, this time for six consecutive games, and it didn't
seem to matter who the opposition was (except for New
England) as we sailed through the season. We beat Philadelphia, Oakland, Seattle, Toronto, Tampa Bay again,
and Washington as we brought our season's point total
to 209 with only one game to go. I had scored six more
goals since the last New England game and now had 32

to Mike's 30. Mike couldn't play in the Teamen's last game so I knew I had won the goalscoring title even before we went to Dallas for our final game.

I managed to score two goals in our 5–3 defeat by the Tornado so I finished with 34 goals and a total of 79 points, both NASL records. All I needed now was to help the Cosmos win the Soccer Bowl and this would be a season comparable to the one I enjoyed in Lazio's championship year.

I could already taste the Soccer Bowl victory champagne as we easily beat Seattle, 5–2, in the one-game first-round playoff. I didn't score but Bogie did; he scored twice in fact. Franz Beckenbauer, Vito Dimitrijevic, and Steve Hunt got the rest.

In the semifinal round we went to Minnesota for the first of a two-game series. Since we had won, 4–2, at Minnesota earlier in the season we weren't too worried about what the outcome would be. What a surprise was in store for us! Charlie George, the English international striker, scored the first goal for Minnesota only 52 seconds after the kickoff. As if that wasn't enough to put us off our stride, Erol Yasin collided with George when he scored and had to leave the game. Jack Brand, not even suspecting he was in for the biggest shock of his career, came in as his replacement. In the 18th minute Steve Hunt inadvertently deflected the ball past Jack and I got the uneasy feeling that nothing was going to go right for us. Then the stylish Alan Willey made it 3–0 with a beautiful goal in the 29th minute. We were down 3–0 in less than 30 minutes; it didn't seem possible after the way we had played during the season that any NASL team could play that much better than us.

In the second half we came out determined to put an end to the embarrassing state of affairs. And we looked as if we would show we were number one when I scored within three minutes of the kickoff. But five minutes later that splendid midfielder Ace Ntsoelengoe made it 4–1. From then on it was all one-way traffic toward our goal. Alan Willey scored four more times in a 20-minute blitzkrieg to set a new playoff goalscoring record of five goals in one game. The final score was an incredible 9–2.

We were a worried group of players on the plane back to New York. Somehow we would have to beat the Kicks twice in the return game at Giants Stadium: once in a regular 90-minute game and then again in a 30-minute minigame. Of course, if the Kicks won the first game there would be no need for the minigame.

There were 60,000 eager fans at Giant Stadium on August 16 and if anyone needed their support it was Jack Brand. Having let in eight of the nine goals scored against us two days earlier Jack must have been reluctant to face the Kicks' goalscoring machine again, but he had no choice since Erol Yasin was still suffering from a mild concussion. Jack needn't have worried—he was brilliant this time, as was our defense. In the first game that night it seemed hard to believe that the two teams out on the field were the same ones that had played in Minnesota. We seemed to have reversed roles—the Kicks were now the worried team. We deserved our 4–0 victory as we put on one of our best performances since I joined the club. Dennis Tueart and I both scored two goals each thanks to some brilliant midfield support from Bogie, Vito Dimitrijevic, and Franz Beckenbauer.

The second game—the 30-minute minigame—was much more even and ended in a 0–0 tie. It was then up to the goalkeepers to prepare themselves for the shootout.

Both teams tried their best in the shootout that day and after playing for 215 minutes the winner was decided when Franz Beckenbauer beat goalie Tino Lettieri in the sixth round. We were in the conference final and the

crowd went wild. Despite our joy I've got to say we felt
sorry to see the Minnesota team eliminated in a flimsy
shootout.

Our conference final was a much simpler task and was
an anticlimax after the scare the Kicks had given us. We
beat Portland 1–0 in Portland and 5–0 in Giants Stadium,
where 65,000 fans joined in the celebration. Dennis Tueart
scored the only goal in the first game and another in the
second. Steve Hunt, Franz Beckenbauer, Seninho, and I
scored the other four.

In the other conference final Tampa Bay beat Fort
Lauderdale, 3–1 and 2–1. Since the Soccer Bowl was to be
held in Giants Stadium we obviously had an advantage
(an unfair one, many critics were quick to claim), but
we really didn't feel we needed an advantage to win as
we were playing a team we had beaten twice before that
season. We controlled the play for most of the game and
even if Rodney Marsh had played (he was injured) I
don't think the Rowdies would have beaten us. Our one-
touch passing had the Rowdies groping right from the
beginning and it was no surprise when we took the lead
in the 30th minute as Dennis Tueart cracked a shot into
the goal off a pass from Steve Hunt. A minute before
halftime I headed in our second goal.

The Rowdies bounced back in the second half, especially during one 10-minute period when they really had
us on the defensive. In the 73rd minute their aggressiveness paid off when Mirandinha, their Brazilian striker,
scored with a hard shot. But that's all they could manage
for our defense was superb, particularly Pino Wilson,
Carlos Alberto, and Werner Roth. Three minutes after
Mirandinha's goal, Franz Beckenbauer waltzed through
the Rowdies' defense and slipped the ball to Dennis
Tueart, who raced into the penalty area and dribbled the
ball past goalie Winston DuBose to make it 3–1.

The game was over 14 minutes later and we were

champs again. The 74,901 fans in the stadium who had cheered the whole 90 minutes gave our team a roaring tribute as we ran our victory lap. As in 1977 there were gallons of champagne in the locker room, and why not? We had enjoyed a near-perfect season. We had broken many NASL season records including: most wins in a season (24); most goals scored (88); and largest total attendance (717,856). Yes, 1978 was a vintage year.

We had little time to relax and savor the glory of our second straight NASL title for the Cosmos team was about to undertake the most unusual, toughest, and longest tour ever attempted by a top pro team in soccer's history. And if the prospect of ten weeks in Europe and South America wasn't enough to dampen our spirits, we had only to remind ourselves of the three all-star exhibition games scheduled before we left.

So three days after the Soccer Bowl, instead of packing bags to take the family to a seaside resort or a country cottage, I was scoring a goal against the World All-Stars (a squad that contained such luminaries as Leao and Rivelino of Brazil; Gallego, Olquin, and Tarantini of Argentina; Boniek, Deyna, and Lato of Poland; Rep and Rijsbergen of Holland; and Cubillas of Peru) at Giants Stadium. Four days later we were back at the stadium, this time to face the fine Spanish club Atletico Madrid. We lost that one, 3–1, and it was obvious that the Cosmos were a little weary after a very tough NASL season. The Spaniards, on the other hand—like the other European teams we were about to meet on the first half of our world tour—were fresh and rested as they were preparing for the opening of their season.

Our third famous guests at Giants Stadium a few days later were the world club champions, Boca Juniors, who were led by my old mentor Juan Carlos Lorenzo. This exciting game ended in a 2–2 tie. But there was no time to celebrate holding the top club team in the world to a tie. Within hours we were boarding a plane at Kennedy Airport for the European part of our tour—seven countries and nine games in 29 days.

The planning of the 1978 tour left much to be desired. The day after we arrived in Munich, jet lag notwithstanding, we played the classy Bayern Munich club, Franz's old team and one of the great powers of European soccer in the seventies. We lost by the embarrassing score of 7-1. We were outrun, outshot, and outclassed all night and to add to our agony there were 79,000 Germans watching our miserable display.

Our rout was blamed on our taking on too much too soon after the season's end, particularly by Eddie Firmani, who criticized the Cosmos executives for allowing the tour to take place at all. On the other hand, of the $600,000 taken at the gate, the Cosmos earned $240,000, a lot of money even by Warner Communications' standards. Throughout the tour I tried to convince many of my teammates and all of the coaching staff how important it was for the Cosmos to earn money during the off-season. Unlike the top foreign pro clubs, most of whom had been around for eighty to one hundred years, we had built the most expensive team in soccer history in less than five years. We certainly couldn't wait ten or twenty years to recoup our multimillion-dollar investment.

Don't get me wrong, no one was more tired than I was before the '78 tour was over. Bayern, Brescia (Italy), Stuttgart (West Germany), Freiburger (West Germany), Chelsea (England), Atletico Madrid (Spain), AEK (Greece), Red Star (Yugoslavia), and Galatasaray (Turkey), all in four weeks, was too much even for a soccer fanatic like me. And there was even more to come. Two weeks after our game in Turkey we were off to South America to play Boca Juniors, Independiente, and other famous clubs in Argentina, Bolivia, Ecuador, and Brazil, a total of seven games in 21 days.

In 1977 we had also taken a long tour but we had been given more time between games and countries and the opposition, apart from Santos and Flamengo in Brazil, couldn't be compared to those teams we faced in 1978. Because the pace was slower and the planning more sensible the team had had the opportunity to enjoy some sightseeing in the countries we visited: China, Japan, India, Venezuela, Trinidad, and Brazil.

Personally, I've never been interested in seeing the touristy spots and I'm probably the only visitor to China who ever turned down an offer to see the Great Wall. I was also the only Cosmos player who didn't visit the Acropolis in Athens during our 1978 tour. I was sitting by the big pool on the roof of the Athens Hilton when Freddie Grgurev and Robert Iarusci, two former Cosmos teammates (and still my two best friends), suggested we get dressed and visit the world-renowned landmark.

"Why should I go there," I replied, "when I can see it from here?"

They left with the rest of the team and I stayed poolside, nibbling on a delicious Greek melon and sipping Chivas Regal. Now if all tourists acted the way I do when I'm overseas none of them would return home worn out and needing another vacation.

Some people got upset when in China in 1977 I refused to eat at public functions where only Chinese food was served. I don't like Chinese food so rather than embarrass our Chinese hosts I simply announced I was not hungry. By the end of our five-day stay in China the friendly Chinese officials assigned to our party were concerned about my health, wondering how "a big man like Mr. Chinaglia" could go through life not eating. I never had the heart to tell them that I was eating all my meals at the Italian Embassy.

That the Cosmos management learned a great deal from our 1977 and 1978 tours was obvious from the way our 1979 tour was planned. First of all, we had eleven days of rest after the season before we left and, just as important, the teams we faced in our tour of the Far East were for the most part easy opponents. From Hong Kong to Australia we drew big crowds. At one game in Djakarta, Indonesia, we played before 85,000 fans, 5,000 more than the previous record for a Cosmos game. On the tour I scored 19 goals, four more than I did in the 1978 tour.

But of all the trips overseas with the Cosmos the one game that stands head and shoulders above the rest was the March 1977 Lazio–Cosmos match in Rome. My three-day stay in Rome was filled with a bittersweet mixture of happiness, nostalgia, and tears as I was given a welcome that would have thrilled even a victorious, returning Caesar.

I remember how excited I was about returning to Italy. I was up all night in the sleeping compartment of the train from Zurich talking to Peppe (who was trying to get some sleep in the bottom bunk). More than the excitement of seeing old friends and familiar sights kept me awake. I was nervous about being arrested on a legal technicality once I reached the border. All too often in recent years wealthy Italians who have emigrated have been arrested upon visiting Italy for not paying some unknown tax or violating some civil law.

Just as I feared, when we reached the border at Chiasso the train stopped and two loud voices shouted, "Where is Chinaglia?" It was the border guards. They were opening up all the compartment doors as they yelled. I got out of bed and looked at Peppe. He seemed even more scared than I was. Finally they reached our compartment. There was a knock on the door. A gruff voice bellowed, "Is Mr. Chinaglia in there?"

It was one in the morning; what a time to have to face the police. I opened the door slowly. Two uniformed guards were outside. One of them pushed the door open all the way, grabbed me in an embrace and kissed me on my cheek. He told me he was a Lazio fan. The other guard also embraced me, only tighter than his colleague. I thought he was going to squeeze out whatever life I had left in me after the scare I'd had. And then I realized the three of us were crying. I was back home in emotional Italy. My three-day crying jag had begun.

At five in the morning we pulled into the Rome station and once again I was frightened for there were thousands of people as far as the eye could see. Before the train had even stopped I realized that many of the crowd were women holding up babies. It didn't take long to discover that all the babies were named Giorgio and the mothers wanted me to kiss them. Since there was no way to get off the train I kissed as many as I could by leaning out the windows. The mothers cried, their babies cried, and naturally I cried.

I then went to the door of the train to wave to the sea of faces even though Peppe was yelling, "Don't go near the door, Giorgio!" Strong hands grabbed me and pulled me off the platform. Lifted onto the broad shoulders of a big fat man I was carried to the Lazio bus that was waiting outside the station. Then, followed by thousands of screaming people, the bus went toward the Grand Hotel.

From the bus window I saw that the graffito "Long Live Chinaglia" still was on some walls. I've got to say I really enjoyed seeing them again. And I got a real kick when the bus driver told everyone aboard that no one had been allowed to sit on the last seat of the back row of the bus (the one that used to be reserved for me) since I left Lazio.

The next day there were thousands of fans waiting for us when we went to practice. My old friends the maintenance workers were also waiting for me, and once again there were kisses and tears. Professor Mazzei told me afterward that he had never seen so much affection for a player expressed by club workers before. One of the ground crew had actually sobbed as he told the professor, "It isn't the same without Giorgio." Naturally, I was deeply touched by this and other sentimental exchanges that morning. When I get emotional I feel weak in both my stomach and legs, and I could see I wasn't going to be of much use to the Cosmos during our game with Lazio. As it was I hardly knew what I was doing out on the field when we played that afternoon, and some of the time I wasn't even certain which team I was playing for. I don't think the fans did either. When I scored a goal for the Cosmos and instinctively ran over to the Lazio section they stood up and cheered as if I had scored for Lazio against Rome. As a matter of fact, they continued to cheer for such a long time the referee asked me to come back to the center circle so the game could resume. Believe me, I really didn't want to leave that Lazio cheering section, with all its warm memories.

We won that game, 2–1, and everyone, including Pino Wilson and the rest of the Lazio team, seemed pleased. That night we went by bus to the Lazio–Cosmos banquet. Hundreds of taxis followed our bus, all of them with their off-duty signs on. While we were eating I rose to my feet to acknowledge a toast from Umberto Lenzini. Instead of making a speech, I asked everyone to "stop eating and listen to me." The Lazio crowd seemed to know what I was going to say and you could hear a pin drop as I continued. "All I want you to do is to sit for one minute and think about two of our friends whom we loved very much." Before I even mentioned the names of Tommaso and Luciano Re Cecconi my voice broke and the Lazio players were crying. (I hadn't intended to ruin the evening but I'm afraid I did.) I then turned to Lenzini and said. "Signore Lenzini, we won't be here for tomorrow's Derby with Rome, but no matter how the team plays I want you to give each player an extra bonus in memory of our departed friends." Lenzini, who was also crying, nodded his head at the suggestion.

During this tearful scene most of the Cosmos players had been looking at each other with perplexed expressions. I think the family atmosphere on the Lazio club surprised them; I'm certain it left a lasting impression on all of them. Robert Irascui said during the ride back to the hotel that it was the most unusual soccer banquet he had ever gone to.

But the Rome trip was not all tears. I took Robert and Shep Messing to Jackie O's to show them how I used to live before I settled down to a quiet suburban life in New Jersey. We had a marvelous time and Shep admitted that if he hadn't seen for himself the royal treatment I received from everyone from the cloakroom attendant to the owner he wouldn't have believed it. After several bottles of Dom Perignon had been consumed he learned that I had been telling the truth when earlier I had told him I wasn't allowed to pay for anything at Jackie O's. It's not often Shep is at a loss for words but when we left that night without getting a check Shep was speechless.

When our visit to Rome ended I found it difficult to leave. I would be lying if I didn't admit I enjoyed every moment of the adulation and affection showered on me. I even enjoyed being besieged by the pushy reporters and the insensitive *paparazzi* who still appeared from the unlikeliest places to annoy me.

For a few days after I returned to New Jersey I was homesick for Rome. During my year in America I had forgotten how it was to be recognized by everyone on the streets, and now I realized I missed it. There was no doubt I also missed the warmth and love that I and my former teammates enjoyed in the rich atmosphere of the Lazio club. But eventually I got over it. As the days went by I had time to reflect upon the difficulties of day-to-day life in Rome, the agony of being separated from my fam-

ily, and how happy Connie and the children were in
America. I also reminded myself that Connie and I were
now able to lead a normal social life for the first time
since our marriage. Whereas in Italy I had unsuccessfully
tried to protect her from the public, in America she
was involved in numerous activities without fear of being
accosted by fans or reporters. One other reason I finally
stopped pining for a way of life that I could never have
again was because I remembered the many new friends
I had found in this country. One of them especially, Steve
Ross, had helped to fill the gap left in my life after the
death of Tommaso.

Today, although I still miss my friends and lifestyle in
Rome, I consider myself a full-fledged American. In the
summer of 1978 I took the oath of citizenship at Hack-
ensack, and I don't think there was ever a prouder man
to receive his citizenship document from a U.S. judge.
I was very pleased to have present at the ceremony Jay Em-
mett, an executive in the Office of the President of Warner
Communications; his executive assistant, Michael Martin;
and Carmen Ferragano, executive assistant to the president.
After the ceremony I dropped Freddie Grgurev off in
Manhattan, then continued toward home. When I reached
the George Washington Bridge I stopped the car and
cried. I think it was the combination of becoming a citizen and the sight of this particular bridge that started
the tears rolling down my cheeks. Ever since I moved to
America I've known that just across the bridge is "home."
It's a feeling I never really had before moving to New
Jersey—at least not since I grew up. Like most professional soccer players, I moved around most of my teenage
and adult life. Permanence is something we players expect
to have only after we retire. Yet I'm totally convinced
that Englewood is "home" now and will continue to be
even if I retire tomorrow.

CHAPTER 11

In 1977 I DECIDED to open a soccer camp for boys and girls. For part of every summer since then it's been held at Suffield Academy in Suffield, Connecticut, and Ramapo College in Mahwah, New Jersey. It was clear to me in '77 that a giant void existed in the area of competent coaching for young Americans. I couldn't do much about the lack of qualified coaching in our high schools and colleges, but I felt I could contribute something during the summer months when the youngsters were on vacation. So with Peppe's help I put together a blueprint for a soccer camp where there would be expert instruction, a great deal of personality building, and lots of just plain old fun. I wanted a camp where the fun part would not be neglected for I believed then, and still do three years later, that if the children have a good time then the coaches and counselors will also have a good time, and if the staff is happy then it follows that the teaching–learning process will be greatly enhanced. That's why a strict, army-like camp with coaches barking orders with all the gentleness of drill sergeants is a miserable camping experience for all concerned.

As for instruction, I insist that we keep it simple for soccer is a simple game. There are camps where the so-called new experts try to make it take on the trappings of American football by using pseudosoccer terminology and spelling out complicated unrealistic pregame plans. But none of that goes on at my camp. Since getting possession and maintaining possession of the ball is really what soccer is all about we concentrate on developing those basic skills. Thus trapping, passing, tackling, ball control, dribbling, shooting, and heading are the skills we practice most of the day. A good camp should not be expected to produce superstars but it should prepare its youngsters for competition. I'm happy to say that our campers leave able to perform the basic skills.

Although we cover every aspect of the game and every position from goalie to winger, my camps seem to attract the youngsters who want to be strikers or center forwards. I realize, of course, that every young soccer player wants to be the one who scores the most goals on his or her team, but I like to think the primary reason for all the would-be center forwards at my camps is that they want to emulate me.

The idolized sports star has a serious obligation to his worshipers. I, for one, take my responsibility very seriously, going out of my way to make certain that youngsters see me only in a favorable light. For example, I can curse and explode in a fit of anger as well as the next man but somehow I control myself whenever there are children around; as far as leading a scandal-free life goes I don't think any special effort on my part has ever been needed. Consequently, when a young boy or girl tells me that he or she wants to be "a center forward just like you, Giorgio," I can feel proud.

Scoring goals is obviously the most exciting part of soccer. Unfortunately, since teams began using the 4–2–4 with its two center backs in the late fifties, scoring goals

has become more and more difficult. The use of the
4–3–3 and 4–4–2 and using sweepers have further complicated the lives of center forwards as teams defend with
seven or more players when using these systems. When I
was a teenager at Swansea I used to enjoy watching old
British soccer movies of the forties and fifties. The most
significant thing I learned from those films was that the
center back (then called the center half) was expected to
control a vast amount of space in the penalty area. No
wonder Tommy Lawton, England's super center forward,
scored so many fine individualistic goals! Once he received a pass near or around the opponent's penalty area
he usually had only one man to beat or to avoid before shooting. Nowadays a center forward not only has to
get past two central defenders blocking the direct route to
the goal, but he also must avoid midfielders and even
forwards who drop back. (It takes some courage to oper-
ate in the opposing penalty area these days—courage not
only to withstand the rough tackles of numerous defenders
but also courage to go for even low-percentage scoring
chances, no matter how many flying legs and bodies are in
the way.)

Probably the most important requirement for a center
forward today is the ability to turn with the ball when
facing the wrong way. To improve this skill we spend a
great deal of time teaching all our youngsters (for all
players find these abilities useful) how to shield the ball
and how to fake their intended direction before turning.

Another skill we try to help the beginner perfect, no
matter what position he plays, is one-touch passing.
Many times a player with his back to the opponent's goal
will elude his markers simply by passing off the ball to a
teammate and then racing away from his opponent so that
he can face the goal when he gets a return pass.

Shooting is another skill that all players must be good at,
but nobody more than the center forward who probably

will shoot twice as much as anyone on his team. I tell all my campers that whenever possible the shot at goal should be kept low and aimed for the inside of the posts since most goalkeepers need more reaction time to reach that kind of shot than one coming at them waist high or higher.

The toughest type of shooting is shooting on the run. Because it's so much harder for youngsters to master than the dead-ball kick many get disheartened. I try to encourage them by telling them about the many shots I've kicked wide or over the bar when kicking on the run. I also remind them that if they want to be top center forwards they've got to be as accurate in their kicking of moving balls as in their kicking of dead balls.

Another skill the top center forward has got to have is the ability to run at top speed with the ball. At our camps we make a special effort to encourage every youngster to spend at least 15 minutes at each practice session running alone with a ball. Most youngsters don't look up while they're running with the ball. This means that they have no idea where their teammates or their opponents are so when they run into difficulties they are usually forced to kick or to pass haphazardly. We try to break them of that habit by having them practice kicking the ball twice as they run, then looking up before the third touch of the ball.

Dribbling is another skill we stress. Dribbling, of course, is more complicated than just running with the ball since the dribbler is moving in different directions at different speeds and the player running with the ball is doing nothing more than getting from one point to another as fast as he can.

In addition to these and other individual skills our camps teach all the fundamentals of the game and, of course, we have coaches specializing in the defensive, midfield, and goalkeeping skills.

What I try to get across to all the players, be they strikers, midfielders, defenders, or goalkeepers, is that the easiest way to go from one place to another on a soccer field is not always to follow a straight line. Soccer is a game where one pass forward and one pass back is quite often the only way to advance and keep possession of the ball. Too many American youngsters are in a hurry when they get onto a soccer field and try to take the shortest route. Because of this most American kids kick the ball as soon as it arrives—and usually as hard as humanly possible. It takes a lot to convince the youngsters that the ball should be handled as softly as possible so that it can be moved from place to place with absolute accuracy. Except when shooting or making a long pass there's no reason in the world why youngsters should be charging into the ball as if they have an argument to settle with it. The ball should be thought of as a friend. As one of my Italian coaches once said, "It should be treated gently if you expect it to do as it's told."

Another fault I find with youngsters at my camp is that, like many American soccer fans, their eyes are always on the ball. Experienced players (and fans too) know that what is happening away from the ball can be just as important as what is happening near the ball. Because they're concentrating so much on the ball youngsters don't see their opponents slipping into open spaces waiting for a pass. And many youngsters fall into the offside trap because they're not watching their opposing defenders.

Our youngsters also need help in learning to move off the ball. Players on top teams are almost always running when one of their teammates has the ball. By moving into the open spaces the experienced players give their teammate who has the ball all kinds of options. They also give the opposing defenders somebody else to worry about and often force the defenders to leave a gap in their defense as they move to mark these players. Probably the most common error youngsters make is passing the ball to a teammate, then, instead of running into position for a return pass, standing still and watching the teammate run on alone without support.

In addition to skills, tactics, and physical conditioning we also try to teach our campers all about at least one team position so that when they leave our camp they will be able to fit into any team they join. Despite the modern trend in pro soccer toward the all-purpose player who can play any position, I firmly believe youngsters should be taught that a back is a back, a midfielder is a midfielder, and a forward, a forward. It doesn't make any sense for a youngster to play as a back, for instance, if he's a weak tackler, no matter how adept he may be in overlapping his forwards. Nor should a delicate artistic type be given the center forward spot.

For fifty to seventy-five years soccer coaches have been spouting clichés about the 11 soccer positions. Surprisingly, many of the old sayings still make sense: "You've got to be a little crazy to play goalie"; "Backs must be strong and fast"; "Center halves [now center backs] must be tall and good in the air"; "Halfbacks [now midfielders] must be able to run 90 minutes nonstop"; "Wingers are the dribblers of the team"; and "The center forward must be built like a tank." There's not much wrong with those old stereotypes except for the obvious fact that today we expect all players to be skillful, even our defenders.

Nowadays a good defender doesn't rely upon sheer strength to stop his opponent. Knowing when to go in for the tackle is often just as important as knowing how to tackle in modern soccer. A skillful back will never rush in when the opponent has the ball at his feet; instead he'll stall his opponent until help comes or until his opponent has either overrun the ball or been forced to pass.

Today's defenders also know that there's no need to mark man-to-man when the ball is in the opponents' half of the field or far away from the penalty area. A player like Wim Rijsbergen, for instance, is too busy helping us by running off the ball when we have it to worry about his opponent. But once we lose possession he will race back to cover his man, staying between our goal and the opponent whenever things get sticky.

As for midfielders, they still do more running than anyone else and they still can be divided into defensive and offensive types just as the old halfbacks of the thirties and forties could. The former still spend more time helping out on defense, the latter, helping the forwards. The main ingredient in a successful midfielder's makeup is the ability to come up with ways to open up the opponent's defense. To accomplish this, midfielders should be the best passers on the team. Of course, if a midfielder can also dribble like a Neesken or a Bogicevic then the odds are he'll be setting up more goals for his forwards.

Although the main job of the center forward and any other striker is to score goals, more and more goals are being scored by midfielders. With the ever present wall of defenders making it tough for the strikers, the midfielders are expected to move into the penalty area and try to score since one of them is often able to get into good shooting position before the opposing defense can mark him.

Unlike the old days when center forwards were often tanks, today's strikers are agile and fast as well as strong and powerful. Most of the time a central striker acts as a targetman for the rest of his team. And everybody knows that his opponents usually have one or two players assigned to mark him tightly.

How much a striker can get away from his markers separates the men from the boys. Gerd Muller's knack for outfoxing his opponents helped him to be the most prolific goalscorer in international soccer of the late sixties and middle seventies. One second there would be two or three defenders breathing down his neck, the next he would be alone with the ball at his feet and only the goalkeeper to beat.

Some strikers who can't shake off their markers resort to taking longer shots. If they can hit a ball from 25 to 30 yards with the accuracy of a Karl Heinz Granitza then it might pay off, but the ball has to be hit with remarkable strength and spin to fool the top modern goalkeeper.

There are other strikers who rely more on their heads than on their feet to score. Those who are successful with their heads usually aim downward when heading, again because goalies have more difficulty with low shots than high ones.

However, even the best soccer camp has yet to figure out a way to teach the instinctive knack that all top strikers have of being in the right place at the right time.

When people ask me what the secret of my success as a striker is, I always answer that I'm at the top because I've had more than my fair share of luck. In soccer if you aren't lucky you should not become a striker. Of course, my critics say that every time I score it's pure luck, but actually to score consistently in modern soccer takes more than *just* luck. You have to have that natural ability for positioning yourself at the right place, you must have total concentration, and you must believe that every time you get the ball you're going to score. The last reason I've been so successful is just as important. I've always been completely dedicated to the game. There have been many better players than me who failed to make it to the top simply because they didn't work as hard as I did.

If you were to ask any former European player what he dislikes most about the NASL nine out of ten would not say the shootout, the fact that there can be no tie games, or even that man-made abomination, artificial grass playing fields. No, the one thing we're nearly unanimous in condemning in the NASL is the long-distance travel involved in our road games. The one, two, and even three thousand miles between franchises is absolutely mind-boggling for those of us used to soccer leagues covering such small areas that a trip of four hundred miles would either put you in another country or into the middle of an ocean.

The long hours spent on road trips are not only a waste of precious time but also both tiring and debilitating for the players. It's no wonder that so few teams play well on the road. In 1979 the Cosmos made trips to San Diego, Tampa, Vancouver, Los Angeles, and Portland. We Cosmos players were thankful that Team Hawaii moved to Tulsa in 1978, saving us a repeat of the 10,000-mile round trip of 1977.

Somehow the NASL must change its scheduling so that more games are played within a smaller area. The present regional setup has very little effect on us because in 1979 24 of our 30 games were with teams in the other five divisions. I think each team should face only others in its division during the regular season, and then those awful road trips would only be necessary at playoff time. I realize that many teams would object if the Cosmos and other attractive teams were no longer available during the regular season to draw the big crowds, but I see no other way to eliminate both the enormous travel time and expense involved when East and West Coast teams visit each other. (A trip to Portland illustrates my point: The air fare alone costs the Cosmos close to $6,000 and the flight via San Francisco takes 7½ hours plus another 2½ hours to and from airports—a total of 10 hours.)

I certainly don't intend to put all the blame for the Cosmos' not winning its third successive NASL championship in 1979 on all those exhausting road trips, but I do feel they were largely responsible for our low morale.

Until Johan Neeskens came onto the team at the end of June we played poorly on the road, even when we won.

We beat Portland, 2–1, but only with the help of a shootout. We then went to Chicago and lost, 3–1. Chicago's a city I've never liked. I suppose it's mainly because the city has so many unhappy memories for me, including one time in 1973 when I had all my luggage stolen in what I was told was a fashionable downtown hotel. The incident occurred after Lazio had faced Pelé and his Santos team at the small Hanson Stadium. As seems to be the case whenever I visit the Windy City, the weather was atrocious, so bad that the near-flood conditions forced the game to be canceled minutes before the kickoff and re-scheduled for the next day: Memorial Day.

We lost, 4–2, before a full house of 12,000 fans. I think Santos was probably the best team Lazio ever played. Pelé had a marvelous game; I played well too, scoring a goal with a 25-yard shot and giving Luigi LaRosa the pass from which he scored.

The next time I went to Chicago was in 1976, a month after I had joined the Cosmos. The Chicago team responded to a record 28,000 turnout by routing us, 4–1, in one of the worst defeats ever suffered by the Cosmos. We all played poorly, especially Pelé and me. Yet the Chicago papers on the following morning had rave notices about Pelé; he was so magnetic that even when he had an off night reporters said he looked good.

This time nothing was stolen but the service at the downtown hotel was downright unfriendly, even rude. People often talk about Chicago's being a friendly city, a big city with small-town charm. Perhaps, but *I* have yet to be convinced that it is anything other than a big raw metropolis with as much charm as its famed grimy Loop has sophistication. Compared to New York, Chicago is the pits.

I was in Chicago again in the winter of 1979 for a sport-

ing goods show at McCormick Place, a vast box-like mon-
strosity on Chicago's lakefront. Perhaps it was because of
the 24 inches of snow on the ground or the wild icy winds
off the lake, but the Chicagoans seemed more unfriendly
than ever. I tried another high-priced hotel but once more
service was so discourteous and sloppy that you couldn't
compare it to a similar-priced New York hotel. The
final depressing memory of this visit to Chicago was the
incompetence of the taxi drivers. Only once out of three
trips did the driver take me to my destination without
asking me the way (as if I would know!), and one driver,
who thought I was some sucker from Britain because of
my Welsh accent when I speak English, claimed that after
midnight he was entitled to double the fare.

After the 1979 Chicago game our dressing room was as
quiet as a funeral parlor since we all knew we had played
terribly. Only reporters searching for quotes wanted to
talk.

It's interesting to note the difference between soccer re-
porting in the United States and in Europe. Whereas European journalists write up their personal observations and
opinions of a game without going near a dressing
room, their American counterparts base much of their
stories on the reflections and views of the coaches and
players. The reason for this difference is, I guess, that most
of our sportswriters are still learning about the sport
which makes them hesitant to diagnose a game without
hearing what the participants have to say about it. Unfortunately, this dependency on quotes defeats one of the
purposes of the dressing room. A dressing room should be
a place where players can calm down and relax. Instead,
the numerous mini–press conferences with NASL players
surrounded by male and often female reporters desperate
to get their stories before deadlines maintain the keyed-up
atmosphere of the game. At Giants Stadium there is really
a tendency toward a hectic dressing room. At some clubs

four or five reporters are common; at the Cosmos' we
sometimes have so many it's difficult to find your locker.

That Chicago game proved to be the last straw as far as
Eddie Firmani was concerned. Two days later he was out
as coach. I think the biggest shock about Eddie's dismissal
was the timing. For quite a while I had had the feeling
that Eddie would be gone at the end of the season.
Actually, I could sense that Eddie wanted to leave. But to
fire a coach in the middle of a season, a coach with a
season's record of 10 wins and 2 losses, was unexpected to
say the least.

Even more surprising was Eddie's subsequent decision
to sign with the New Jersey Americans of the American
Soccer League. Now I've got nothing against the efforts of
the ASL to become a worthy competitor to the NASL but
right now it's strictly a semiprofessional league with little
improvement made since commissioner Bob Cousy announced in 1975 that the ASL was on the verge of becoming a major soccer league.

Eddie should have been more patient. With his credentials he could have had the pick of the NASL teams if
only he had waited awhile. Or he might have gone to
Britain where I'm sure many teams would have jumped
at the chance to hire him. Moving from the top team in
the United States to the bottom team of the Eastern Division of the ASL was probably the biggest mistake he ever
made in his soccer coaching career. Within a few months
he left the Americans to take over the Philadelphia Fury
in the NASL.

Eddie was replaced by Ray Klivecka, our assistant coach.
Having Ray carry on was a wise decision, as was the decision to persuade Professor Julio Mazzei to become techni-
cal director because the professor had the experience Ray
lacked. The professor had learned a good deal in his
eighteen years with Pelé, Santos, and the Brazilian national team. One of his strengths was his mastery of tactics

and set plays, and we had always been weak on set plays, probably because it was hard for our coaches (even Eddie, who was first-rate), to handle so many top stars who felt they knew more than the coaches did. With the professor it wouldn't be that easy for us to flaunt our international experience since his background was second to none. He was, after all, a trainer and an assistant coach with Santos during its heyday in the mid-sixties, when it was undoubtedly the best team in the world and arguably the *crème de la crème* to appear in the thirty-odd years since World War II.

But on our next road trip we played even worse. Although we narrowly beat Tulsa, 3–2 (after being down 2–0 in the second half), we were hammered by Vancouver, 4–1, and then lost to Minnesota, 3–2. By the middle of June we were a worried team and it took a magnificent display by Johan Neeskens in his first game with us to give us back some of our confidence. Within a few weeks we looked a whole lot better than we had in the spring. Johan's nonstop running and aggressiveness had inspired all our team members to work harder, the very thing I had been hoping for all season long. Once he settled down, the Cosmos won eight games in a row and scored 30 goals while playing great soccer.

But I thought the best game we played that season was before Johan arrived. It was when we hosted the full Argentinian national team in an exhibition match before a huge crowd of 70,000 fans. Advance sales for the game were the best since Pelé's farewell game and we expected a full house. We would have had an overflow if there hadn't been massive traffic jams on the roads that circle the stadium. Thousands of fans were still stuck in their cars hours after the match had started.

The atmosphere at the stadium was as electrifying as at any World Cup final. There seemed to be thousands of Argentinians waving blue and white flags and wearing blue and white shirts and hats. All of a sudden, what had been just a midweek exhibition game became a showdown between the top American team and the top world national team. The crowds really supported us and I'm happy to say we rose to the occasion.

Fresh from their successful European tour with victories over Holland and Scotland and a tie with Italy, the Argentinians probably did not expect to face a psyched-up Cosmos team playing 4–4–2 for the first time and playing as if it were competing for the World Cup.

The Argentinians, who received a thunderous welcome as they lined up, had the following starters: Ubaldo Fillol in goal; Jorge Olguin, Miguel Oviedo, Daniel Passarella, and Alberto Tarantini on defense; Juan Barba, Americo Gallego, and Diego Maradona in midfield; and Rene Housema, Leopoldo Luque, and Daniel Valencia on the forward line.

Our starting team was Jack Brand, Bobby Smith, Wim Rijsbergen, Carlos Alberto, Santiago Formoso, Rick Davis, Francisco Marinho, Antonio Carbognani, Dennis Tueart, Mark Liveric, and myself.

I played as a withdrawn center forward with Dennis and Mark ahead of me. We played a counterattacking game and it nearly worked. For 88 minutes we held the world champion team to a 0–0 score. The Argentinians had possession of the ball at least 65 percent of the time but their offensive thrusts petered out against our defense. Carlos Alberto had the game of his life, as did Ricky Davis who neutralized Diego Maradona, the 18-year-old Argentinian soccer sensation. Bobby Smith bottled up winger Daniel Valencia. As a matter of fact, Ricky and Bobby handled those two international stars as if they were unknown American rookies.

By the middle of the second half I was convinced we could win the game. Our counterattacks were proving more dangerous than the clever but slow buildup of the champs. Marinho came close once and I nearly scored with a long shot. Then I made what I thought was one of the most important goals of my life only to have the referee, Gino D'Ippolito, call it back because of an offside. A few minutes later I passed the ball to Marinho who took a hard shot. Ubaldo Fillol couldn't hold it and it came to me on the edge of the penalty area. Fillol came racing out of his goal to confront me. I chipped it over his head into the goal, but again I was unlucky because Miguel Oviedo rushed back to the goal line and headed the ball away just in time.

Then it happened. With less than two minutes left to play, Bobby fouled Daniel Valencia out on the left wing and the latter's free kick floated across our goal to the head of Daniel Passarella who scored with a powerful header. Antonio Carbognani appealed to the referee, claiming Passarella pulled him down as he went up to head the ball, but the referee ignored his protest.

Although we lost, 1–0, we felt it was a marvelous evening for both the team and the fans. It was a real team performance; we had all extended ourselves, much more than at any other season game. In a way I think we all felt like celebrating after that match, that's how happy we were. I for one couldn't remember a Cosmos game which I enjoyed playing in more. I had particularly liked roaming around the midfield launching attacks as I used to do at Lazio. I know I had a fine game. My booing section must have thought so too. For once they were silent all evening.

I consider that Cosmos–Argentina match to be one of the three most memorable games of my career—the other two being my first international appearance for Italy in 1972 and the Lazio–Foggia game in 1974 when we won the championship.

But the 1979 season was to hold few other happy moments and lots of disappointments. One letdown was my failure to take my third goalscoring title even though I was leading the goalscorers all through the season. My failure was mostly due to a groin injury (the first serious injury in my career) which forced me to sit out a number of games in late July and early August. Still, it was an exciting finish. By the last day of the regular season the Argentinian striker Oscar Fabbiani of Tampa was only one point behind me. He had 57 points to my 58.

There was one game left for each of us on that important Sunday in August. Tampa was to play Detroit and we were going against Washington.

Sadly, that morning my groin injury still bothered me. I didn't know what to do. I wanted to play if at all possible because if I didn't and Oscar scored against Detroit he would take the title. Still undecided, I drove to Giants Stadium early in the afternoon. The weather was atrocious; heavy rain was leaving puddles on the astroturf. I knew as soon as I saw the field that I would be crazy to play under such conditions. It was no longer just a question of withstanding pain. If I played on that slippery turf, one fall or one clumsy tackle might keep me out of the playoffs. Was the chance of scoring a goal and gaining the title worth taking such a risk? I still wasn't sure.

The professor and Ray had already decided to rest three of our regular starters in preparation for the playoffs since the Washington game no longer had any bearing on our playoff position. They were kind enough to let me decide whether to play or not. It was obvious that they were all for my retaining the goalscoring title, and for this I will always be grateful. But when the time for decision making came it was clear to me that I owed it to the team and the Cosmos organization as a whole to make sure I was healthy and available for the playoffs. Winning our third straight championship was far more important than my winning an individual honor. I told the professor and Ray that I wouldn't play. I think I did the right thing.

As I had feared all along, Oscar scored a goal and with it won the goalscoring title. My only consolation was the fact that I had scored 26 goals to his 25.

An even bigger disappointment was our loss to Vancouver in the National Conference final, which was also one of the two semifinals of the playoffs.

To reach the National Conference final we had beaten Toronto, 3–1 and 2–0, in the first round of the playoffs and in doing so ran our winning streak to 10 games. In the second round we were surprisingly beaten, 3–0, at Tulsa, which meant we had to win both the regular and the minigame at Giants Stadium. And we did—3–0 in the first game and 3–1 in the minigame! We won both by playing the best soccer I have seen the Cosmos produce since our 1976 game against Los Angeles. As Tulsa's coach Alan Hinton said, "It was world-class soccer at its finest."

We then traveled to Vancouver for the first game in the conference final. Playing without the injured Wim Rijsbergen and Johan Neeskens we were beaten, 2–0. To make the evening a complete catastrophe, Eskandarian and Carlos Alberto got themselves into serious trouble. First Eskandarian, for reasons unknown even to himself, deliberately charged into Kevin Hector with only eight seconds left in the game. He was given a red card (and rightly so, for no matter how badly a game is going I believe a clear foul must be penalized). His ejection meant he could not play in the return match at Giants Stadium. Then Carlos Alberto, of all people, began arguing with the officials as they left the field. He threw his shirt at the referee and allegedly spat at the linesman. The next day he was suspended for the rest of the season by the NASL even though there was no hearing on the matter. This unusual (and undemocratic) suspension was immediately challenged by the Cosmos. When nothing was resolved our club filed a lawsuit against the league.

Despite facing a team that had beaten us three times in 1979 without two of our starting defenders we felt we could beat Vancouver twice in one afternoon. We were hoping for, and expecting, a 70,000+ crowd which would bring out our best just as it had in our matches with Tulsa and Argentina.

Unfortunately, the fans let us down that Saturday, September 1. Only 44,000 showed up, a small crowd for such an important game. I guess the pleasant summer day might have made the beaches and parks irresistible but it's more likely that many of our fans stayed home to watch the game on television. (ABC allowed its nationwide TV coverage to be shown in the New York–New Jersey area.) Whatever the reason for the empty seats on the upper deck my teammates and I were really disappointed. Surely all those missing fans hadn't given up on us already? Had they forgotten what a lift it gives us to see and hear a full house of enthusiastic Cosmos fans? So we were one game down, but our chances of winning were still good.

Vancouver's well organized and talented team lined up as follows: Phil Parkes, the number one goalkeeper in the league; Buzz Parsons and Bob Lenarduzzi, two fine Canadian defenders playing alongside two former English first-division center backs, John Craven and Roger Kenyon; three English players in midfield—Ray Lewington, Carl Valentine, and Alan Ball, the former English national team captain; and three international strikers in Kevin Hector, Trevor Whymark, and Willie Johnston. It was a very impressive lineup.

In goal for us was Hubert Birkenmeir, the West German who had come to us during midseason and made the goalkeeping position his own with some splendid performances. Our defenders were Nelsi Morais, who had re-signed with the Cosmos during the summer when half of our players were injured, Wim Rijsbergen, Franz Becken-bauer, and Marinho; the midfield spots were assigned to Johan Neeskens, Bogie, and Ricky Davis; and up front were Seninho, Dennis Tueart, and me.

For the first 15 minutes it was all Cosmos. So much so that I had the eerie feeling that the Whitecaps were hold-ing themselves back. Their usual emphasis on frantic speed was nowhere to be seen. Instead their players were concentrating on slow methodical buildups and only oc-casionally mounting fast attacks down the sidelines. Even Kevin Hector, their great striker, appeared to be loafing.

In the 10th minute Bogie ran toward the center of the Vancouver defense drawing John Craven away from me. I moved to the right side of the penalty area and just as I expected Bogie pushed the ball to me. I took a few steps then hit it hard and low from about 15 yards out past the onrushing Phil Parkes. We were one up, the first time we had taken the lead in a Vancouver game all season.

The game had been so one-sided up to then that all of us, including the roaring, happy fans, were convinced that at last we would teach the Whitecaps a lesson. And even though they tied the score a few minutes later we still had the better of the play. Their goal came after Wim Rijsbergen fouled Willie Johnston just outside the right side of the penalty area. A deceptively slow, curling free kick from the foot of Alan Ball went over everyone's head and met the outstretched foot of John Craven who had raced to the left side of the goal. His shot flashed past Hubert in goal.

Our midfield continued to dictate the pace of the game. Bogie, Johan Neeskens, and Ricky Davis were continually feeding balls to Dennis Tueart, Seninho, and me. Seninho was having a superb game; he was causing the Vancouver defense trouble every time he received the ball. In the 38th minute he dribbled past three opponents, stopped near the goal line, then flicked the ball across the Vancouver goal where I was waiting to flick it past Phil Parkes. We were now leading 2–1, and looked good.

A few minutes after the halftime Seninho again raced through the Whitecaps' defense, but this time I failed to hit his through pass properly and Phil Parkes had no trouble saving the shot. We missed some other chances to score as well but we appeared to have the first game well in hand even though Dennis Tueart had been forced to leave the game because of an injury. Midway through the second half Johan Neeskens also had to go off. Once he left our offense was no longer as good and the Whitecaps' defense was able to contain our forwards. Nevertheless, we were still winning, 2–1, with less than five minutes to go. I suppose most of us were already thinking about the minigame which was to follow when Carl Valentine set off on a long run down the left wing. He crossed a fast low ball which rose no higher than three feet. Before Hubert could catch it Willie Johnston made a diving header to put in the equalizer.

The regulation time came to an end with the score 2–2. We then played 15 minutes of overtime without any scoring although we came close twice in the last three minutes. I had a header knocked over the bar by Phil Parkes, then Boris Bandov saw his shot kicked off the line by Alan Ball.

We were both disappointed and frightened—disappointed at having to go into a shootout after controlling most of the 105-minute game and frightened when we realized that if we lost we wouldn't be going to the Soccer Bowl.

I sat down on the bench having vowed earlier in the season not to get involved in shootouts again. And since I was 0–4 I had yet to hear any of my teammates object. Not only do I dislike shootouts but I find it agonizing to watch them. This was never more true than on September 8 when so much rode on a handful of kicks.

Thankfully, we came through the shootout with a win, having had three successful attempts to Vancouver's one.

The 30-minute game that followed was far different from the first game of the afternoon. The Whitecaps moved onto the offensive much more than they had in the previous 105 minutes. They also appeared more lively in the minigame than they had earlier. I had been right, they had slowed down their usual fast pace in the first game. Their coach, Tony Waiters, must have assumed there would be a minigame. It was clever tactics on his part for we found ourselves struggling at times to keep up with their speed, particularly whenever their young English midfielder, Carl Valentine, set out on one of his lightning runs into our penalty area from the midfield. In the 15th minute he took a long shot that hit the crossbar and bounced down onto the goal line. At first the linesman waved for a goal, claiming it had gone completely over the line before bouncing out, but he changed his mind when questioned by the referee. We had a goal disallowed when, with less than two minutes to go, Mark Liveric dribbled past Bob Bolito, the Whitecap substitute, and kicked the ball into the goal. The referee said Mark pushed Bolito, a decision Mark objected to violently but with no luck.

So after 30 minutes we were still tied, 0–0. Once more we were forced into a shootout.

By this time most of the starters who had played for 135 minutes were ready to collapse. We had been on the field since two o'clock and it was now five-thirty-five. Nevertheless, the shootout sequence was probably one of the most exciting moments in NASL history. With so much riding on the result there was drama attached to every movement of the players. The crowd noise softened to a hush as the kicker approached the ball. Then there was an explosion of sound as the goalkeeper saved or the kicker scored.

Unfortunately, Vancouver scored three goals to our two in the five rounds of the shootout—and we were no longer in the playoffs.

It was hard to accept that defeat because I still felt we were the best team in the league during 1979, and I must admit I took it very hard. My teammates know from experience that when we lose I'm practically incommunicado unless I score. But that day, even though I had put away two goals bringing my playoff total to six goals in six games, my scoring didn't make me feel like talking.

I never apologize to anyone for being so intense about soccer or so determined about achieving success in whatever I do. Nor do I pretend to be happy when I'm down in the dumps because of a loss or a poor performance. On the other hand, I don't expect anyone to feel sorry for me when I'm in one of my postgame depressions. I knew that my teammates would shake off the blues within a few hours, or perhaps a day at the most. For me, it would take at least five or six days of brooding before I would feel right again. I don't know why defeats affect me this way and believe me it's no picnic taking life so seriously, but there's no changing one's nature and I've given up trying.

CHAPTER 12

SATURDAY, NOVEMBER 10, 1979, was one of the happiest days of my life in America. That was the day I helped my friend Freddie Grgurev celebrate his signing a lucrative contract with the Philadelphia Fever of the MISL (Major Indoor Soccer League). I got a terrific kick from Freddie's impressive contract, not just because he was being paid more money than he had ever seen in his life before but because he had proven that he had star status. In 1978 when the Cosmos had let him go to Rochester, Freddie's career looked as if it had already peaked, but he played well with Rochester and was the top goalscorer in the first MISL season during the winter of 1978–79.

After he signed the contract Freddie and I enjoyed a good bottle of Dom Perignon at the Apollo Restaurant on top of the Sheraton Heights in Hasbrouck Heights, the hotel the Cosmos use for the team and its opponents. During our dinner we were joined by the owners of the hotel, Art Sherman and Nick Nicolosi, both of whom have become big soccer fans since the Cosmos moved to Giants Stadium. While we were discussing how well the MISL had done in its first season and the way it had

shown the NASL a thing or two on how to promote indoor soccer, Peppe arrived with the early edition of the
New York Times. In it Alex Yannis reported that I had
been offered $500,000 to play for the New York Arrows of
the MISL, and that I had turned it down.

The story was, insofar as it went, accurate for I had been
approached many times throughout the summer of 1979
by executives of the MISL about my availability to play
in the 1979–80 season. What the article didn't mention was
that one club that had contacted Peppe had offered me $2
million for a three-year contract. But I had said no to all
the tempting offers, even though I would have loved to
play soccer during the long winter months. My main reason for refusing was that I felt it a matter of principle not
to split my allegiance between one club and another even
if it were only for four months. I also saw some conflict
of interest involved in playing for both of the rival soccer
leagues, particularly since the NASL had also scheduled
an indoor tournament during the winter months. Furthermore, I knew that if I played for the Arrows, the Cosmos
would be concerned throughout the indoor season that I
might get injured and thus not be available for the 1980
opener. And I too would worry about not being fit to play
in the NASL.

There was also a more selfish motive behind my refusing the MISL offer—I want to remain with the Cosmos organization after I retire and I wouldn't dream of doing
anything that might interfere with my chances. The
Cosmos have come a long way in the last few years and I
want to be here to help with their continued growth.

Since 1976 I like to think I have done my part in helping the club achieve its enviable position in world soccer.
As an official of the organization, I think I would be in an
even better position to guide the club as it tries to become
the best team in the world. Of course, some people have
already described me as the only playing general manager

in the NASL. If by that they mean I make numerous sug-
gestions (even when they're not requested) or that I'm
willing to pick up the phone and call any of the Cosmos
board members in situations where a younger player or a
less famous senior player would be reluctant to do so, then
I suppose they're right. Actually, what many of my critics
don't understand is that as a company Warners expects its
employees to show initiative. So if I get an idea they expect me to bring it up without being asked. Furthermore,
if I think some particular thing should be done or believe
that some particular matter is being poorly handled, I feel
it's my duty to speak up.

I have no doubt whatsoever that the Cosmos will be
the strongest club in international soccer in the next
decade. The reason why we have been so successful up to
now is our willingness to spend money on buying players
and then keeping the players happy once we get them.
With so many world-class stars on one team it's easy to
understand why the name "Cosmos" has become synony-
mous with the word "soccer."

I suppose there's a parallel between the Cosmos and the
Yankees in this respect. You can go to the back roads of
middle America and ask people what comes to mind
when you say the word "baseball" and seven out of ten
will answer—the Yankees. The same would apply to the
Cosmos and soccer except the response would be more like
nine out of ten. Overseas the story would be the same.
This is not to say that the Yankees and the Cosmos are the
best baseball and soccer teams in the United States.
Neither of us won championships in 1979 despite our
overpowering rosters but we do enjoy a glamor that none
of our rivals share. Both clubs dominate the headlines
when we're playing and are constantly involved in some
controversy or other. The Cosmos and the Yankees players
and executives also project an exciting image off the field
as well as on. And another interesting parallel is the fact

that neither George Steinbrenner nor Warner Communications takes any money out of the club's income.

It could be said, too, that both clubs use the same high-powered merchandising approach to selling a sport. Of course, the Cosmos, being a relatively new club, have to do many things differently from the Yankees. We've had to act like a new exclusive store opening up on a street filled with many other fancy stores. We had to go out and find the best "merchandise" to lure the potential customer into our "store." And once we had attracted some customers we had to continue to bring in more desirable "goods."

Now that we've built up a huge following, I believe it's going to be even more difficult to keep these fans happy. There are few great players left in the world whose coming to America will excite the fans the way a Pelé, a Beckenbauer, or a Neeskens did. This means that the Cosmos will have to devote even more of their money and energies to consolidating the talent they now have and to producing their own junior talent. This is exactly where I think I can be of some help to the club. I know what's needed to develop American soccer talent and what's wrong with our present setup not only at the Cosmos but also throughout the country.

First of all, we must do something about the coaches in both high schools and colleges. Quite often, some of our youngsters know more about the game than their coaches do. It's not that our coaches don't want to learn, it's just that we expect men (and women) who have never played soccer to learn from books and clinics how to teach the finer points of the game. And even those coaches who have played at high school and college can't teach soccer properly, because what kind of soccer are they used to? Probably the American style of "kick and run" which until recently was taught in all American schools.

Then, of course, there's the problem of what to do about the short school season; two or three months in the fall is not enough to produce good soccer players. By the time a youngster has reached high school he should be playing the game every day for at least nine months in the year if he's going to become a pro.

Obviously, the answer to the high school and college problem is for the NASL clubs to start their own junior teams where kids from the age of 12 to 17 can be under the constant supervision of experts. When the best of them graduate from high school, they should sign professionally with the clubs and pursue their college studies during the off-season.

It's no accident that only a few of the hundreds of college players drafted into the NASL at the age of 22 or 23 have achieved fame in our league. Except for goalkeepers, almost all the material now coming out of our colleges is pitiful. The NASL college draft is not worth the effort or the time that goes into it. It will do only as a stopgap measure to make sure that all NASL teams have their three Americans on the field at all times as the rules call for, but I'm afraid that in the long run it will only lower the standards of play in the NASL.

Another aspect of high school and college soccer that is discouraging is the continued use of unlimited substitution. Unlimited substitution over the age of 14 is detrimental to good soccer on two major counts. First, it breaks up the rhythm of the game with the constant interruptions for substitutions. Second, it encourages an emphasis on powerhouse soccer, since as soon as players are tired the coach brings on fresh bodies. This means that the young American doesn't learn how to pace himself during a game. It also means that any time he makes a mistake or tries to be inventive and do something a little different he can expect to be taken out of the game. Because of these pressures, you seldom see young high school or college players who are willing to dribble with the ball. Not that our coaches would encourage individualism even if there weren't unlimited substitution. In American schools any player who is unorthodox is usually considered a nonteam man by his coach. Unfortunately, from what I have seen, most American coaches want to produce big, strong robots programmed to do little more than run, kick, and run.

Another drawback to the progress of the young American soccer players is the enormous amount of drugs used in the schools, particularly among the high school generation. What scares me more than anything else is that so many kids consider taking drugs a normal part of life. I've talked to lots of kids about drugs and when I suggest that drugs and soccer don't mix they imply that I'm out of touch with modern America since "everyone is into drugs." Furthermore, they say, "What about all the pro soccer players who drink alcohol?"

Most players, in fact, do drink, especially after a game when they unwind, but most stick to beer, which can easily be absorbed by the body of an athlete who trains as hard as a pro soccer player. Even my own taste for good scotch and champagne has not affected my fine physical condition, nor I hope my mental faculties, though I must admit I probably have to practice harder than the beer-drinking player to retain my fitness and much harder than players who don't drink at all. The moral here, of course, is that if you're going to drink do it in moderation and be prepared to run a little harder in practice than your nondrinking teammates.

But drugs are a far different matter. They not only disrupt the biological processes but also leave devastating scars on the mind. And from what I've seen it seems obvious that many of our younger American players in the league have dabbled with drugs. Although our society is still debating the legalization of certain drugs I, for one, feel they have no part in soccer and would like to see the NASL initiate dope tests like many foreign leagues already have. And I think it has to be done now, before more and more American youngsters replace the NASL's imported players during the NASL's Americanization in the 1980s. With the frightening rise in drug use in our high schools and colleges, I predict the NASL will find that drugs will be as difficult a problem to solve as the inadequate coaching being offered to our youth.

Actually, even the coaching in the NASL is not all that good. The lack of coaching continuity might be one of the reasons. How can the NASL expect to attract and retain famous coaches when every time a team loses three to four games the owners begin thinking about replacing the coach! In 1979 alone nine coaches were fired. There are 24 teams in the NASL; only one can win the championship. Does this mean that 23 coaches have failed every year? Believe it or not, many of our club owners feel they have.

What bothers me most about all this changing of coaches is that many coaches, fearful about losing their jobs, fill their teams with defensive players. The resulting dull games can't help but bore all the new fans coming out to see the "new sport" for themselves. That undermines all the excellent missionary work of the NASL publicists and marketing people. All I can say is thank heavens there are teams like the Tampa Bay Rowdies, the Fort Lauderdale Strikers, and the Minnesota Kicks. These clubs understand how to present attractive attacking soccer and make a profit at the same time.

Just as bad as defensive soccer is for the league's future is the poor caliber of referees officiating at NASL games. The sad thing about the deplorable standards of officiating in the league is that the league office is aware of the problem but sees fit to ignore it. The Cosmos have repeatedly offered to pay up to 50 percent of the cost of hiring top international officials without any response from the league. The problem will have to be faced, and soon. We need world-class referees immediately because the American and Canadian officials have been out of their depth ever since the NASL started to attract top international players.

Our present officials fail in two respects. In the first place, they're not always able to spot fouls as they're either 30 or 40 yards behind the play or they're not quick enough to observe the slyly executed ones. Some of our more experienced European and South American defenders really know how to get away with things, as the Cosmos' artistic ball handlers will attest. It was not surprising in 1979 that our team with so many elegant and artistic players received more than our fair share of hacking, elbowing, butting, and pushing.

The second failure of our referees is that when they do see fouls they often ignore them. The offended player and his teammates, taking the view that the referee has lost control of the game, then resort to violence themselves out of frustration (and, at times, in self-defense). How can anyone blame them? The referee situation is a disgrace.

As a result of the many inferior aspects of American soccer, from coaching to refereeing, it's going to take at least another decade before our national team can begin to compete successfully against the top teams in the World Cup. Although I believe the United States Soccer Federation (USSF) has finally seen the light and provided real money for coaching and international tours there's a lot of work to be done before we take our rightful place in world soccer.

I think the present U.S. national team coach, Walt Chwzowych, has done a fine job with what he had to work with. Those who feel we should go out and hire a top foreign coach are missing the whole point about the development of an American team. It's essential that the coach, whoever he is, and the players must grow together. Cesar Menotti of Argentina, Jupp Derwall of West Germany, or Enzo Bearzot of Italy might bring to our team some more understanding of tactics and strategy but none of them could have much success with the type of player now available in the United States.

Few critics will deny the fact that most American-born players are noticeably short of top-class skills. I can only think of three who have shown signs of achieving greatness: Ricky Davis and Gary Ethrington of the Cosmos and Sonny Askew of Washington. Top goalkeepers, on the other hand, seem to be plentiful in the United States. Shep Messing, Bob Rigby, Dave Brcic, Arnie Mausser, and Alan Mayer can hold their own with most. Unfortunately, goalkeepers are a very specialized part of soccer; their skills have little in common with those of their teammates. I suppose you could say goalkeepers don't really play soccer at all but a mixture of basketball and handball with a little kicking mixed in.

I only hope I'm able to play a part in improving the quality of American soccer. Since I have no intention of leaving America when I retire, I will be able to make myself available to the U.S. national team or any youth team that requests my help. I intend to repay soccer for all the glorious years it has given me and I want to be among the vanguard of American pioneers helping American soccer's advance in the next quarter of a century. Just as I have treasured every moment of my playing career—the joy of championship victories, the honor of representing my country, the warmth of lasting friendships (and even the bitter disappointments and the tears)—so I believe I will enjoy another career in soccer just as rewarding when I retire. But that's another story.

APPENDIX

Giorgio Chinaglia
Born: Carrara, Italy, January 24, 1947
Height: 6'1"
Weight: 185 pounds
Striker

North American Soccer League Statistics

Year	Club	Games	Minutes	Goals	Assists	Points
1976	Cosmos	19	1725	19	11	49 *
1977	Cosmos	24	2217	15	8	38
1978	Cosmos	30	2713	34 *†	11	79 *†
1979	Cosmos	27	2376	26	5	57
	TOTALS	100	9031	94	35	223

NASL Playoffs

Year	Club	Games	Minutes	Goals	Assists	Points
1976	Cosmos	2	180	0	0	0
1977	Cosmos	6	551	9 †	2	20 †
1978	Cosmos	6	540	5	2	12
1979	Cosmos	6	541	6	2	14
	TOTALS	20	1812	20 †	6	46 †

*Led League
†NASL Record

Complete List of Goals with Cosmos

	1976	**1977**	**1978**	**1979**
Regular Season	19	15	34	26
Playoffs	0	9	5	6
Exhibitions	5	21	21	31
TOTALS	24	45	60	63

SUM TOTAL: 192

Previous Pro Stats
Massesse (Div. C, Italy, 1966–67, 32 games): 5 goals
Internapoli (Div. C, Italy, 1967–69, 66 games): 25 goals
Lazio (Div. A, 1969–76, 209 games): 98 goals
Other goal-scoring: Italian National Team (11)
　　　　　　　　　　UEFA Cup (11)
　　　　　　　　　　Italian Cup (11)
　　　　　　　　　　International Cups (20)
　　　　　　　　　　Swansea (29)
　　　　　　　　　　Pre-Cosmos Exhibitions (80)

Cosmos Individual Records
NASL Regular Season
Most Games
Season: 30 (1978); tied with Vladislav Bogicevic
Most Goals
Game: 5 (vs. Miami, 8/10/76)
Season: 34 (1978)
Career: 94 (1976–79, 100 games)
Most Assists
Career: 35 (1976–79, 100 games)
Miscellaneous
Most Consecutive Games Scoring a Goal
5 (6/18/78–7/2/78; 7 goals)
Most Points
Game: 12 (vs. Miami, 8/10/76; 5 goals, 2 assists)
Season: 79 (1978)
Career: 223 (1976–1979, 100 games)
Most Shots
Game: 15 (vs. St. Louis, 7/2/76)

Season: 170 (1978)
Career: 543 (1976–79, 100 games)
Most Minutes Played
Season: 2713 (1978, 30 games)
Most Consecutive Games Scoring a Point
10 (5/28/78–7/2/78; 13 goals, 5 assists)
Most Goals All Games (Including regular season, playoffs, exhibitions)
192 (1976–79)